WILLIE GEARY "BUNK" JOHNSON

The New Iberia Years

Austin M. Sonnier, Jr.

D1563026

CRESCENDO PUBLISHING

NEW YORK

Library of Congress Catalog Card Number: 76-16330

ISBN: 0-87597-102-4

Printed in the United States of America.

FOR NELLIE, AUSTIN III, AND DAVID

CONTENTS

Photographs follow pages 14, 39 and transcriptions.

A real musician is like the note B natural in the treble clef. No matter how the sheet music is turned around it remains B natural. No matter how a musician's life gets turned around he is still a musician.

—WILLIE GEARY "BUNK" JOHNSON

PART ONE

DIDN'T HE RAMBLE

Willie Geary "Bunk" Johnson was born on December 27, 1880 in the city of New Orleans to Thresa Jeffereson and Wm. Johnson. He was, by his own account, one of fourteen children. He began the study of music at the age of seven and one year later, started on the cornet with Professor Wallace Cutchey. According to Bunk, after about a year he progressed to the point that his mother was forced to buy him a cheap cornet at the insistence of Professor Cutchey.

At fifteen, Bunk left school and got his first job as a professional musician playing with Adam Oliver's orchestra. Oliver was a full-time bandleader and trumpeter, and was the first to employ Bunk and pianist Tony Jackson. The orchestra played from score and it was there that Bunk learned the fundamentals of ensemble playing.

In 1895, after about a year with Oliver's orchestra, Bunk joined King Buddy Bolden's band. As Bolden's group played mainly by ear, Bunk preferred that to the stock arrangements of Oliver's orchestra, and he decided to accept the position with Bolden as second cornetist. Very little is known about Buddy Bolden. He was born in New Orleans in 1868 and began playing sometime before 1892. He and a crippled guitar player, Charlie Galloway, composed some of their own music. Players from Galloway's band worked with Bolden, and Edward Clem, Galloway's cornet player, usually filled in for Bolden when Bolden couldn't appear. Bolden's first band was a quartet with Frankie Lewis, clarinet; Brock Mumford, guitar; and Jimmy Johnson, bass. When Bunk joined, the band featured Cornelius Tilman, drums; Willy Cornish, trombone; Bolden, cornet; Willie Warner, clarinet; Brock Mumford, guitar; and Jimmie Johnson, bass. Bolden played everywhere, sometimes more than one job a night. He would go from one band to the other, playing his specialties. As his repertoire of blues was very small—only a few songs—he would play polkas, mazurkas, two-steps, and quadrilles the remaing time. He first played "Make Me a Pallet on the Floor" in 1894. Other tunes included "Bucket's Got a Hole in It", "If You Don't Get No Cake", and his classic, "Funky Butt". He is said to have recorded several cylindrical discs but they have never been found. King Bolden was a nervous, overly aggressive man who drank heavily and kept several women. He wrote and edited his own scandal sheet, *The Cricket*, cut hair part-time, booked his own band jobs, and arranged his own publicity. His bawdy lifestyle diminished him as a musician after twelve years. Syphilis caused insanity and he was committed to the East Louisiana State Hospital where he died in November, 1931.

Bunk stayed with Bolden until 1898, and left to play with the Bob Russell Band. But Russell's band was mediocre, and after a few months Bunk returned to Bolden. By this time, Bolden added trombonist Frank Dusen to the band in place of Willy Cornish. Bunk remained with Bolden for about seven months.

In early 1900, Bunk played at Frankie Spano's club with Jelly Roll Morton, piano, and Jim Parker, drums. He also played with Jelly Roll at Hattie Rogers' sporting house. During this period he played with an assortment of orchestras and brass bands in and near New Orleans, including Tom Anderson's famed dance hall. He also played with pianist-vocalist Mamie Desdoumes.

The next few years were spent on the road with minstrel companies and a circus. Bunk was with the P. G. Loral Circus from about 1900 to 1902. He also played with McCabe's Minstrel, directing the band and playing cornet. Arthur Marshall was with McCabe at that time. He played piano in the shows and cymbals in the parades, under Bunk's direction. During this period, Bunk traveled extensively, from Texas to New York and in 1905 to San Francisco.

By 1910, Bunk was back in New Orleans, playing with Billy Marrero's Superior Orchestra. Members included Buddy Johnson, trombone; Louis "Big Eye" Nelson, clarinet; Walter Brundy, drums; Richard Payne, guitar; and Peter Bocage, violin. Peter Bocage helped Bunk with his music. He stayed with the Superior Orchestra until 1911 when cornetist Nenny Coycault replaced him when Bunk left to join Frank Dusen's Eagle Band.

Bunk reached the zenith of his career between 1911 and 1914, when he played with the Eagle Band, which was really the old Buddy Bolden Band under the direction of Frank Dusen. Besides Dusen, on trombone, members included Henry Zeno, drums; Dandy Lewis, bass; Sidney Bechet, clarinet; and Brock Mumford, guitar. It was Bunk who influenced Bechet to join. Headquarters for the band was a business establishment on South Rampart and Perdido Streets, called the Eagle Saloon. The band took their name from the saloon. Every Saturday night at the Masonic Hall was Eagle Band Night. The music on Saturday night had to be "hot". And that was the only way the Eagle Band knew how to play. They became

4

the most popular uptown band at that time. A handbill advertising an Eagle Band dance proclaimed:

> The Eagle Boys fly high
> And never lose a feather
> If you miss this dance
> You'll have the blues forever—

When they had a parade, Bunk would put on his brown uniform and Eagle hat and lead the band.

After a while, Bunk began drinking and left Dusen to work in the cabarets in the Red Light District (Storyville). He worked at Lala's across the street from Manuel Parez. For a night's work from 8 P.M. to 4 A.M. he was paid up to $2 and free wine. The tips sometimes ran as high as $15 a night. Occasionally, Bunk played with John Robichaux's orchestra, which for years was the "name band" in New Orleans and in constant demand. They were engaged at the most desirable spots in the city, including the Grunewald (now the Roosevelt) and Antoine's. Each Monday evening, Robichaux appeared at the Masonic Hall in uptown New Orleans where he played in all styles of music, from quadrilles to rag. Bunk was well known for his "sweet" tone, refined taste, and near perfect execution. This was, by far, his best musical period. Tours with trombone player Jack Carey took Bunk through most of the small towns in southwest Louisiana. At a dance in New Iberia he played "Casey Jones" and excited the people to the extent that they wanted to carry him around the hall on their shoulders. When Bunk was playing with brass bands in the uptown section of New Orleans, young Louis Armstrong would steal away from home and follow him. He wanted Bunk to show him how to play the cornet and teach him the blues and other "hot" pieces. According to Bunk, when he was playing at Dago Tony's on Perdido and Franklin Streets, Louis would slip in and "fool around" with his cornet at every opportunity. Bunk showed him how to hold it and place it to his mouth. He also demonstrated the blues. During this time, Bunk played with at least fourteen bands, including some of the best in New Orleans.

In 1914, Bunk left New Orleans permanently. He toured almost constantly but did not play in Chicago where, beginning in 1913 on, jazz began to reach a new audience. This turned out to be an important factor in his musical growth and national acceptance. Joe Oliver, Louis Armstrong, and Freddie Keppard all went to Chicago and became famous. Bunk's time was yet to come. He taught in Mandeville for a year, managing the Fritz Family Orchestra. He then joined the orchestra at the Colonial Hotel in Bogalusa. In 1916 he was in the Royal Orchestra in Lake Charles and a year later, with Walter Brundy in Baton Rouge. For a few years he traveled with the Georgia Smart Set, a vaudeville-minstrel show, and with the Vernon Brothers Circus. In the 1920s he played with Evan Thomas' Black Eagle Band in Crowley, and with Gus Fortinet's Banner Band in New Iberia, Louisiana. The Black Eagle Band members included Joe Avery, Bob Thomas, or Harrison Brazlee, trombone; Robert Goby, sax; Abbey "Chinee" Foster or Walter Thomas, drums; Abraham Martin, banjo; Lawrence Duhé or George Lewis, clarinet; Harold Potier, trumpet; Minor Decou and Sam Dutrey, clarinet.

By 1920, Bunk chose New Iberia as his permanent place of residence. After a few years there he married Maude Fortinet, daughter of bandleader Gus Fortinet. His days were spent jobbing, his nights playing. He remained there until the summer of 1942, when jazz enthusiasts David Stuart, Bill Colburn, Hal McIntyre, William Russell and Gene Williams "discovered" him.

The years from 1920 to 1942 were difficult for Bunk. Things were at a low ebb. New Iberia, a small southern town, did not offer ideal conditions and circumstances for a Negro. Because he lacked a formal education, he had to work at menial jobs to provide for his family. He worked where he could find it—in rice and sugarcane fields; driving trucks and working in a Tabasco sauce plant. Musically, things were not much better. During this period he began to lose the inspiration to play and he suffered physically from bad teeth.

On occasion Bunk led his own band, employing such capable New Iberia musicians as Hypolite Potier on trumpet and Auguste Fournet on trombone. He played small dance jobs in the New Iberia and Lafayette areas. One of his better jobs was with the house band at the American Theatre in Houston, Texas, which featured such singers as Ma Rainey. Most of his work, however, was with the Black Eagle Band and the Banner Band. It was during this time that he developed the well-known "second cornet" style.

Their individual talents were best displayed in this band which allowed for improvisation and originality and did not confine them to the limits of a musical score. They played blues, jazz, and the popular tunes of the day. Solos began with variations on a theme and they expanded, depending on the emotions of the player. The overall approach was not unlike that of the New Orleans dance bands.

When work for the Black Eagles was slow, Evan Thomas played in Gus Fortinet's Banner Band in New Iberia. He was on first trumpet and Bunk on second. The "second cornet" style, on employing a lighter touch, was exploited to its fullest by Bunk. Management used any "excuse" to keep him in the second chair line trumpet position, knowing that it was there that he was at his best. His innate ability at melodic invention combined with a crisp tone and faultless phasing were hard to

6

surpass. Evan Thomas, on the other hand, was a trumpeter in the King Oliver mold. He used a greater variety of tone quality, was forceful, and could be very loud. Trumpeter Harold Potier recalls: "Bunk had some teeth missing right in the front of his mouth—two of them. When we would go on the job, he would take a piece of string and tie it real good to fill the gap. Tie it to his teeth, you know. That was really something. Then he would blow his horn like no other trumpet player I ever heard. That man was too much."

Bunk ventured to Kansas City in 1931 for a date at a place called the Yellow Front Cafe. He played with pianist Sammy Price, singer Julie Lee and drummer Baby Lovett. This was of brief duration and he was soon back in New Iberia with the Black Eagle and Banner Bands.

Gus Fortinet's Banner Band was the leading society band in New Iberia from 1910 to the mid-1930s. Like the Black Eagle Band, they never played in New Orleans. Most of their engagements were in the small southern towns of Louisiana and East Texas. They were, by far, the most musical and commercially successful ensemble to play outside the city of New Orleans. The reason for this was the high degree of musicianship within the band. Lawrence Duhé worked with the Banner Band as did Evan Thomas and clarinetist-saxophonist Morris Dauphine, who had worked with Oscar Celestine in New Orleans a few years earlier. Gus's daughter, Mercedes, studied music at Xavier University in New Orleans, and joined the band when she was sixteen years old. She later married Harold Potier, a trumpet player who spent most of his musical career with the band. Other members included Tom Edward, tenor sax and string bass; Ed Redum, vocal and banjo; Robert Staffort, drums; Wilfred Bocage, soprano and alto sax; and Gus Fortinet, Jr., tenor sax.

New Iberia was, at that time, a hotbed of jazz musicians. There was an awareness not unlike that which existed in New Orleans, and new styles were slowly evolving. There were a few jobs available at funerals and parades, but most work existed in night-clubs and at sponsored dances.

Harold Potier remembers one in particular: "When we played for the Catholic schools, the nuns would ask for your sheet music for a few days before the dance. They would go through it and pick out all the fast tunes. You could not play sentimental numbers, and the blues was out of the question. All they wanted was fast tunes—did not want the kids to get too close—know what I mean? That was hard work, man."

As the leader of the best band in the area, Fortinet was offered more jobs than he could accept. Work was so plentiful there was no reason to rehearse. Anyone playing with the Banner did not need another job to survive.

7

Within this context, Bunk was able to function as he did in New Orleans. He could once again play music that had substance and appeal. There were no critics—at least none like those that were, in later years, to criticize and determine what was financially "best" for him to play. The time was small, but the music was as large and personal as any in which Bunk could possibly wish to indulge. He now felt secure. However, a tragic event was soon to occur which would affect him deeply.

In 1932, while playing a dance in Rayne, Louisiana, with the Black Eagle Band, Bunk and George Lewis witnessed the murder of Evan Thomas. It was a tragedy that would haunt Bunk for the rest of his life. After Evan ran from the nightclub mortally wounded, his attacker, John Gilbey, went completely berserk, and proceeded to wreck the bandstand, smashing most of the instruments, including Bunk's horn. As Bunk said later, they were lucky to get away with their lives. This incident marked the end of Bunk's career for about ten years.

For four years he worked with the New Iberia Parish School Board as a music teacher under the WPA program. He was instrumental in teaching young and aspiring musicians the basics for a successful career. His work included private lessons, directing ensembles and teaching music theory. When the WPA laid him off, he worked as a truck driver, hauling sugar cane for $1.50 a day. He also worked as a laborer for various businesses in New Iberia. This continued to be Bunk's way of life. There was nothing musical for him to do at this time. The Depression had affected everyone so there was no money to pay musicians.

In New Orleans, the best bands were reduced to "pick-up" groups. With the exception of the Eureka, the brass band idiom had almost disappeared. When Joe Payne died, the Excelsior died. The Onward Brass Band ceased when Manuel Parez retired. There were only a handful of small neighborhood bars that were able to hire bands with three or four pieces. Emile Barnes was at the Harmony Inn. Louis Nelson at Luthjen's and George Lewis at Mannie's. The E.R.A. Band, a federal music project that consisted of both professional and non-professional musicians, was phased out by 1937. In order to make a living, musicians accepted any work that was available.

In 1937 a group of jazz critics and enthusiasts, led by Frederic Ramsey, Jr., Charles Edward Smith, Stephen W. Smith, and William Russell, were planning the first book on American jazz. While gathering material, William Russell learned of Bunk from Louis Armstrong and Clarence William. Armstrong met Bunk while playing in New Iberia just the year before. He could not attest to Bunk's recent abilities but remembered his as one of the first men to play jazz in New Orleans. With this in mind, Russell wrote to Bunk in New Iberia and they were soon in-

8

volved in an extensive and fruitful correspondence. Although Bunk provided Russell with a vast amount of information about early New Orleans jazz and musicians, his primary objective was to play his horn again. He made his intentions clear by informing Russell that if he could get some teeth and a horn he was sure he could play. He felt he still had the talent to do a good job.

In the winter of 1942, mainly through the efforts of Russell and his friends, Bunk had his new teeth. He also received a trumpet that was personally selected by Louis Armstrong. Bunk began to practice diligently. He soon recaptured those expressive musical qualities which had made him famous. That spring, he sent Russell a recording of "Maple Leaf Rag" along with a letter stating that he was ready to play again. No one was particularly impressed with his performance on the recording. However, David Stuart, proprietor of the Jazz Man Record Shop in Los Angeles, contacted Bill Colburn and disc jockey Hal McIntyre in San Francisco, to ask them to accompany him to New Iberia to see Bunk and make arrangements to record him. After getting enthusiastic response from McIntyre and Colburn, Stuart called William Russell in Pittsburgh and Eugene Williams in New York. Both agreed to meet Stuart in New Iberia.

On June 4, 1942, Stuart, Colburn and McIntyre arrived in New Iberia. They rented a house, refreshed themselves, and then went to Bunk's house. They were skeptical. They expected to find an old man, probably too weak to play, who could only suggest what the music was like during Buddy Bolden's time. They were pleasantly surprised. Bunk was lively, energetic and articulate. His facility for playing the trumpet and his remarkable memory of past events dispelled their doubts. They were quite satisfied with what they saw and heard.

William Russell and Eugene Williams arrived the following day, and plans were made for the recording session. They left for New Orleans and Bunk was to follow in a few days.

After much time and effort was spent finding sidemen, locating recording equipment, and so forth, they finally assembled at Grunewald's Music Store on June 11, 1942. Ernest Rogers, the drummer, worked in an iron foundry and wasn't available until 3 P.M.; Grunewald's closed at six. That left only three hours in which to work. Twelve acetates, a makeshift studio, intense heat, and street noises created something less than ideal recording conditions. There was no time for rehearsals and no retakes could be made. In spite of all these obstacles, the session was remarkably successful. Bunk recorded nine sides with George Lewis, clarinet; Jim Robinson, trombone; Walter Decou, piano; Lawrence Marrero, banjo; Austin Young, bass; and Ernest Rogers, drums.

9

A rebirth of Bunk's career was underway. The old man was at last doing the thing he loved most. He gained a new vitality. He felt younger and acted that way. In the eyes of his friends he could do no wrong. He was now at his peak—the master. He was the most knowledgeable source of information about a music that had been neglected for nearly twenty years. Bunk was unquestionably one of the most important figures ever to appear on the jazz scene.

His approach to jazz was basically similar to that of Jelly Roll Morton—dynamically restrained, using considerable shading and avoiding the use of the high register. He considered the melody the most important musical element and had a complete understanding of the piano accompaniment in complementing the songs that he played.

Shortly after the initial recording session, Eugene Williams returned to New Orleans and recorded Bunk a second time. The recording took place in San Jacinto Hall. This time they were able to rehearse before the discs were made. Twelve sides were released on the Jazz Information label. Despite the very poor fidelity of these recordings, they were a sensation. Bunk's material included: "When I Leave the World Behind", "Yaaka Hula Hickey Dula", and a version of "Shine", in which he played a phase obviously borrowed from Louis Armstrong's version. Bunk was very relaxed. At times he would simply drop out of the ensemble for a chorus or two. This was not a known practice in New Orleans jazz but probably could be attributed to the fact that Bunk was not particularly impressed with the group.

The next event in Bunk's comeback took place in San Francisco, a hotbed of New Orleans revivalism. In the spring of 1943, Rudi Blesh, a San Francisco interior decorator who was reading a series of lectures on early New Orleans jazz at the Museum of Art, wanted Bunk to play a series of concerts in conjunction with his lectures. Blesh asked for contributions to bring Bunk there, and then asked William Russell how to contact Bunk. Blesh also located a pianist named Bertha Gonsoulin, who had played with King Oliver in Oakland in 1920, and who had known Jelly Roll Morton at Mary's Place. She had given up jazz for church music but was to play with Bunk. Blesh used Lu Watters' sidemen to complete the group.

Bunk left for San Francisco in April. The train was crowded so he was compelled to sit on his trumpet case in the aisle. Trumpeter Mutt Carey, who was working on the train as a porter, recognized him. He had known Bunk in New Orleans before the First World War. When they reached Los Angeles, Carey found him a place to spend the night. On his arrival in San Francisco, Bunk explained that his luggage had been stolen along with his hotel reservation. If the rehearsal was brief it did not hinder the concert, which was quite successful. Bunk was ingratiating and the audience loved him. There was an active interest in traditional jazz in San Francisco and arrangements were made for Bunk to play Sunday afternoons at a longshoremen's union hall. The accompanying musicians included members of the Yerba Buena Jazz Band.

Almost from the beginning there were racial difficulties with the musicians' union and others involved with the jazz scene. Bunk created problems within the band by· insisting that they play the latest hit tunes. The Yerba Buena men had spent years fighting for the acceptance of traditional jazz, basing their style on older recordings. They weren't happy with Bunk's attitude. His drinking had also become a problem. He was scheduled to do a show for the BBC called "Portraits of American Cities", with Herbert Marshall as the narrator. But Bunk did not show up, and at the last minute, Ellis Horn and pianist Paul Lingle hired a studio trumpeter and wrote a melody similar to what Bunk might have played.

David Rosenbaum, founder of the San Francisco Hot Jazz Society, produced some recordings of Bunk with Lu Watters' associates. This group made several interesting recordings. One unique recording features Bunk as a vocalist. In an effort to convince Sister Lottie Peavie, the gospel singer, that it would not be a sacrilege to sing "Down by the Riverside" with a jazz band, he recorded it in a hoarse, throaty rendition, with phrases reminiscent of his own horn work. There is also a moving and beautiful rendition of "Careless Love", and a rollicking and spirited version of "The Girls Go Crazy 'Bout the Way I Ride". These recordings, available on the Good Time Jazz label, have an entirely different sound from those made with the Lewis-Robinson group. The phrasing, rhythm, and dynamics have little in common with the latter.

Due to the trouble over the racially mixed band, Bunk turned to local jobs, working on the waterfront lifting oil cans, and then as a stock clerk for McKesson and Robbins. In July, 1944, he became disillusioned with conditions in San Francisco, and decided to return to New Iberia.

On his way home, he stopped in Los Angeles to record for the World Transcription Service, a subsidiary of Decca Records. He succeeded in making several fairly good recordings, including a previously unrecorded New Orleans work, "Spicy Advice". Bunk's tone is captured here more clearly than on many of his other records. Although this session was notable for portraying added phases of Bunk's style, his work was limited by his problems.

Back in New Orleans, he made a series of recordings for William Russell in 1944 on the American Music label. Baby Dodds and George Lewis were in the band. That fall, the National Jazz Foundation, organized in New Orleans to preserve and promote jazz, sponsored a concert.

11

Bunk played aboard a horse-drawn wagon which advertised the concert, but he did not play in the concert itself. A few months later, *Esquire* Magazine sponsored a similar concert at the Municipal Auditorium. Louis Armstrong, Sidney Bechet, and J. C. Higgenbotham were featured. It was to be a broadcast climaxed by a performance of "Basin Street Blues" featuring the Armstrong group and Bunk Johnson. But due to long, rambling speeches, there was only time for a few choruses by the ensemble. However, recordings of Armstrong and Bunk in instrumental interplay and later with Bunk accompanying Louis' vocal are considered genuine collectors' discs. After the show went off the air, the two of them continued to play together, but were not recorded.

Bunk had given Sidney Bechet one of his first jobs, so in March, 1945, Bechet asked Bunk to join him in Boston. The group included Fred Moore, drums; Pops Foster, bass; and Hank Duncan, piano. They played at the Savoy Cafe. It turned out to be a disaster. Recordings made at the time reveal Bunk playing with poor intonation and missing many notes. He said later that he felt Bechet's soprano saxophone competed with his trumpet but he could not persuade Bechet to play only clarinet They also had differences over the music and Bunk further complicated matters by his drinking. Bechet felt that Eugene Williams kept prodding Bunk to be his own boss, and encouraged him to drink and carouse. Bunk left the band after a few nights. Somehow they did manage, before he left, to make a recording which was issued on the Blue Note label.

What was to follow next in Bunk's career generated the most publicity and success, along with the greatest frustrations of his life. Through the efforts of Eugene Williams, arrangements were made for him to lead a dance band at the Stuyvesant Casino, on the Lower East Side of New York City. The band was to be the Lewis-Robinson group, and was to include Baby Dodds. Bunk agreed, but indicated that, although he wanted to play for dancing, he preferred a different kind of music to that which these men were accustomed. He did not prevail, however, and the band was scheduled to open on September 28, 1945. He remained persistent in his efforts toward change, as he wanted Sandy Williams to replace Jim Robinson. He did not like Baby Dodds' explosive style, either. Still no one agreed with him. Soon, as fate would have it, the band became one of the most controversial groups in the country. There were articles about Bunk and other members of the band in many of the larger magazines, and the major recording companies, including Victor and Decca, sought to record them.

That job ended four months later. However, the manager of the Stuyvesant Casino arranged for Bunk to return. But he also insisted on the Lewis-Robinson band. Bunk was able, after much persuasion, to get

12

pianist Don Ewell, Kaiser Marshall, and drummer Alphonso Steele in the band. The engagement began on April 10, after George Lewis had gotten Bunk sober enough to travel and retrieved his horn from a pawnshop. They continued until May 31, 1946, when troubles within the band came to a head. Bunk had said publicly that the other members of the band were second-rate musicians. He also made a practice of sleeping on the job.

Finally, two sessions were recorded in which the "old master" was able to demonstrate musically what he had in mind. The first of these sessions included a group of tunes recorded with a trio consisting of Alphonse Steele on drums, and Don Ewell, a disciple of Jelly Roll Morton, on piano. These men were part of the Lewis-Robinson group. The reason for the trio was that if there were not sufficient musicians to form a full band, there would not be any other instruments that could detract from the idea Bunk was attempting to deliver. The idea was a good one. The second and more successful session, particularly from the standpoint of those concerned about a recording that would fully display Bunk's talents, was with a group of New York musicians who worked with him in the fall of 1947. They undoubtedly came closer to meeting his requirements than any other group with which he had been associated since he returned to music. These final recordings of Bunk were of a very high musical quality and gave wide dimension to his interpretation of jazz and what jazz should be. These were recorded on the Columbia label. Here, at last, Bunk was presented on records at a time when he was in good health, was at least content with his fellow musicians, and most important, had been playing sufficiently so that his embouchure was in good shape. The recordings were made from December 23 to 26, 1947, in the Carnegie Recital Hall, a small auditorium in the Carnegie Hall building.

The original plan was to put them out as singles, get them into juke boxes, and test the response of the public to Bunk's music. But the test was never made. The records were not released until 1952, when George Avakian produced them on Columbia Records. Without those recordings, the heritage of Bunk Johnson would have suffered. The quality of the music on those recordings was such as to change one's overall impression of Bunk's playing. The listener is now able to view his other records differently. He was an important guiding light in the early years of jazz. But it may be said that his later work was to be his most important and most significant achievement.

A week after the recordings were made, Bunk went home to New Iberia. He remained active playing with local bands including jobs with the remnants of the Banner Band. Because of his teeth, which continued to give him trouble, he chose to play tuba, but he was not very good. By this time, he was a petulant, spiteful man who drank too much and played only when he was in the mood. Bunk waited many years for success, and when it finally came, he was too old and broken to enjoy it.

The only known photograph of Buddy Bolden and his band. Back row: Jimmie Johnson (string bass, bass horn), Bolden (coronet), Willy Cornish (valve trombone), Willy Warner (clarinet). Front row: Brock Mumford (guitar), Frank Lewis (clarinet).

The Superior Orchestra in 1910. Back row: Buddy Johnson, Bunk Johnson, "Big Eye" Louis Nelson, Billy Marrero. Front row: Walter Brundy, Peter Bocage, Richard Payne.

This rare photo of Frankie Dusen was taken in New Orleans about 1900.
(Courtesy Harold Potier)

The Silver Leaf Orchestra in 1911. Left to right: Willie Carter, Hypolite Charles, Sam Dutrey, Sr., Albert Batiste, Philip Nickerson, and Jimmy Johnson. The regular trombone player, Honore Dutrey, was in Baton Rouge on business and didn't return in time to be included in the photograph. (Courtesy Hypolite Charles.)

The John Robichaux Orchestra in 1913, St. Catherine's Hall, New Orleans. Bunk played off and on with Robichaux during this period. Left to right: Walter Brundy, Vic Gaspard, Andrew Kimball, Charlie McCurtis, John Robichaux, Coochie Martin, Henry Kimball, Sr.

Hypolite Charles in 1911.   (Courtesy Hypolite Charles)

Joe "King" Oliver, before he left New Orleans.

Sidney Bechet at 19,
just before going to Chicago.

Bunk in 1942.

The Bunk Johnson Band in New York, 1945. Back row: Jim Robinson, Bunk Johnson, Alcide "Slow Drag" Pavageau, Lawrence Marrero. Front Row: Warren "Baby" Dodds, Alton Purnell, George Lewis.

Members of Bunk's band advertise jazz concert, January, 1945.

J. C. Higginbotham, Louis Armstrong, and Sidney Bechet at the New Orleans Municipal Auditorium in January, 1945. Bunk was on the same program. He and Armstrong played together, but the segment was not recorded.

The Sidney Bechet Quintet, Spring, 1945. Left to right: Fred Moore, Pops Foster, Bunk Johnson, Bechet, Hank Duncan.

At the Stuyvesant Casino, September, 1945. Left to right: Robinson, Pavageau, Bunk, Dodds, Lewis, Purnell, Marrero.

Ma Rainey.

arinetist George Lewis.

Lawrence Marrero, George Lewis and Bunk.

At San Jacinto Dance Hall, New Orleans.

Bunk and Louis Armstrong.

In New Orleans, 1949.

DISCOGRAPHY

The discography lists all the recordings made by Bunk Johnson, whether on 78 rpm shellac discs or long-playing albums, which have been offered for sale since 1942. Many of these recordings are now out of print but occasionally out-of-print recordings are reissued.

Acetates or tapes of broadcasts, private recordings, and recordings made for radio stations are not included here.

Only the original matrix numbers are stated, and all release numbers have been included for recordings issued in Europe and the United States.

INSTRUMENTAL ABBREVIATIONS

ah	alto horn	p	piano
b	bass	sou	sousaphone
bh	baritone horn	tb	trombone
bj	banjo	tp	trumpet
cl	clarinet	ts	tenor saxophone
cnt	cornet	tu	tuba
dr	drums	vcl	vocal, vocalist
g	guitar		

BUNK JOHNSON'S ORIGINAL SUPERIOR BAND

Bunk Johnson (tp), Jim Robinson (tb), George Lewis (cl), Walter Decou (p), Lawrence Marrero (bj), Austin Young (b), Ernest Rogers (dr).
Recorded: New Orleans, June 11, 1942

MLP132 Yes Lord I'm Crippled .... Jazz Man (B) 17; Jazz Man (E) (B)
MLP133 Down by the River .... Jazz Man 8; Folkways FP57, FJ2803; Jazz Man (E) 8
MLB134 Storyville Blues .. Jazz Man 10; Gazell 1033; Embassy 130
MLB135 Weary Blues .... Jazz Man 9, Jazz Man (E) 9; Gazell 1012
MLB136 Bunk's Blues .... Jazz Man 10; Gazell 1033; Embassy 130
MLB137 Moose March .... Jazz Man 9, Jazz Man (E) 9; Gazell 1012
MLB138 Pallet on the Floor .... Jazz Man 16
MLB139 Ballin' the Jack .... Jazz Man 16
MLB140 Panama .... Jazz Man 8, Jazz Man (E) 8

Bunk Johnson talking, same session.

MLB141 Bunk's Life Story, I ... Jazz Man (A), Jazz Man (E) (A)
MLB142 Bunk's Life Story, II .... Jazz Man (B), Jazz Man (E) (B)
MLB143 Bunk's Life Story, III ... Jazz Man (A), Jazz Man (E) (A)

All titles from this session are also on Good Time Jazz M12048; Vocalion (E) LAG545; Mandadisc (E) (no catalog number).

MLB132-141-142 and 143 were issued on Jazz Man and Jazz Man (E) 78's without any catalog numbers. (A) and (B) shows the coupling. MLP133 to MLB140 were issued on Jazz Man (E) lp without a catalog number.

BUNK JOHNSON'S JAZZ BAND

Bunk Johnson (tp), Albert Warner (tb), George Lewis (cl), Walter Decou (p), Lawrence Marrero (bj), Chester Zardis (b), Edgar Mosely (dr).
Recorded: New Orleans, October 2, 1942

4657-1A Big Chief Battle Axe .... Purist 1004
4657-1B Big Chief Battle Axe .... Jazz Information 13; Commodore 657 CEP80, DL30007; Jazztone J717
4658-2A Dusty Rag · .... Jazz Information 14; Commodore 658 CEP80, DL30007; Jazztone J1013
4659-3A Franklin Street Blues .... Jazz Information 12; Commodore 656 CEP 79, DL30007; Jazztone J1013
4659-3B Franklin Street Blues .... Purist 1004
4660-4A The Thriller Rag .... Jazz Information 11; Commodore 655 CEP79, DL30007; Jazztone J1013
4661-5A Sobbin' Blues No. 2 .... Jazz Information 16; Commodore 660 DL30007; Jazztone J717, J1212
4661-5B Sobbin' Blues No. 1 .... Jazz Information 14; Commodore 658 CEP80, DL30007; Jazztone J1013, J1212
4662-6A When I Leave the World .... Jazz Information 11; Commodore 655 CEP79, DL30007; Jazztone J1013, J1212
4663-7A Sometimes My Burden .... Jazz Information 16; Commodore 660 DL 30007 Jazztone J1013, J1212
4664-8A Bluebells Goodbye .. Jazz Information 13; Commodore 657 CEP80, DL30007; Jazztone J717, J1212
4665-9A Shine .... Jazz Information 15; Commodore 659 DL30007; Jazztone J1013, J1212
4666-10A Yuaka Hula Hickey Dula .... Jazz Information 15; Commodore 659 DL30007; Jazztone J717
4667-11A Weary Blues .... Jazz Information 12; Commodore 656 CEP79; Jazztone J1013

All titles from DL30007 are also on Mainstream M56039, S6039; Melodisc (British) MLP12-112; Top Rank (Dutch) HJA6505; Vogue (French) INT40027.

BUNK JOHNSON
Bunk Johnson (talking and whistling)
Recorded: New Orleans, 1942
Bolden's Style .... American Music LP643
Funeral Parades ... American Music LP643
Tony Jackson ... American Music LP643
Pete Lala and Dago Tony ... American Music LP643
(piano solo) same session
Maple Leaf Rag . American Music LP643
Baby I'd Love To See You ... American Music LP643
Bunk Johnson (tp), Bertha Gonsoulin (p).
Recorded: San Francisco, April 11, 1943
Maple Leaf Rag .... Not issued
Bunk's Blues ... Not issued
High Society .... Not issued
Stardust .... Not issued
Pallet on the Floor (take 1) ... American Music LP643
Pallet on the Floor (take 2) ... American Music LP643
Pallet on the Floor (take 3) .... Not issued
Pallet on the Floor (take 4) ... American Music LP643

BUNK JOHNSON AND THE YERBA BUENA JAZZ BAND
Bunk Johnson (tp, vcl), Turk Murphy (tb), Ellis Horne (cl), Burt Bales (p),
Pat Patton (bj), Squire Girsback (b, tu), Clancy Hayes (dr, vcl), Sister Lotta
Peavey (vcl).
Recorded: San Francisco, January - February, 1944
RM401 Ace in the Hole   Jay 5; Good Time Jazz 34, LP17; Vogue (British)
       GV 2181; Jazz Collector N2, JS860; Cavatone 350
RM402 Careless Love .... Jay 5; Good Time Jazz 63, EP1016, LP17; Vogue
       (British) GV2182; Jazz Collector N2, JS864
       2:19 Blues ... Cavatone 350; Good Time Jazz 34, LP17; Vogue (British)
       GV2181, JS860
       Nobody's Fault But Mine ... Good Time Jazz 37; EP1016, LP17; Vogue
       (British) GV2176
       When I Move to the Sky ... Good Time Jazz 37, EP1016, LP17; Vogue
       (British) GV2176
       The Girls Go Crazy ... Good Time Jazz 38, LP17; Vogue (British)
       GV2212, JS861
       Ory's Creole Trombone ... Good Time Jazz 38, LP17; Vogue (British)
       GV2212, JS861
       Down by the Riverside ... Good Time Jazz 63, EP1016, LP17; Vogue
       (British) GV2182, JS864
       Dusty Rag   Not issued
       Maryland, My Maryland ... Not issued
       Milenberg Joys . Not issued
       Of All the Wrongs ... Not issued
       South .... Not issued
       Do You Ever Think of Me ... Not issued
   All selections from GTJ-LP17 are also on Good Time Jazz L12024; Vogue
(British) LDG110, LAG12121; Vogue (French) LD198.

BUNK JOHNSON'S V-DISC VETERANS

Bunk Johnson (tp), Floyd O'Brien (tb), Wade Whaley (cl), Fred Washington (p), Frank Piasley (g), Red Callender (b), Lee Young (dr).
Recorded: Los Angeles, July 11, 1944
Spicy Advice .... Gar 2502; Purist 1001, LPP101; VJM VEP33
Arkansas Blues .... Gar 2502; Purist 1001, LPP101; VJM VEP33
Ballin' the Jack .... Purist LPP101; VJM VEP33
Lowdown Blues .... Purist LPP101; VJM VEP33
Mama's Gone Goodbye .... Purist LPP101
Careless Love Blues .... Purist LPP101
I Ain't Gonna Give Nobody .... Purist LPP101
Panama .... Purist LPP101
Alexander's Ragtime Band   Not issued
     All selections were originally recorded for World Record Transcriptions.

BUNK JOHNSON'S BAND

Bunk Johnson (tp), Jim Robinson (tb), George Lewis (cl), Lawrence Marrero (bj), Alcide "Slow Drag" Pavageau (b), Sidney "Jim Little" Brown (tu), Warren "Baby" Dodds (dr).
Recorded: New Orleans, July 30, 1944
106   I Don't Walk Without You .... Not issued
109   St. Louis Blues .... Not issued
110   Lowdown Blues ... American Music LP647, 253; Storyville SLP128

Same personnel; Myrtle Jones (vcl) replaces Sidney "Jim Little" Brown.
Recorded: New Orleans, July 31, 1944
201   San Jacinto Stomp .... American Music LP645; Storyville SLP127
202   Sister Kate .... Not issued
203   Sister Kate .... Not issued
204   Sister Kate .... Not issued
205   Blue As I Can Be .... Rejected
205½   Blue As I Can Be .... Rejected
206   Blue As I Can Be .... American Music LP647; Storyville SLP205
207   See See Rider .... Storyville SLP205
208   Precious Love .... Storyville SLP205
209   Life Will Be Sweeter Some Day .... Not issued
210   Life Will Be Sweeter Some Day   Storyville SLP128
211   St. Louis Blues .... American Music 252; Storyville SLP152
212   Tiger Rag .... American Music Baby Dodds No. 4 (never issued)
213   Tiger Rag .... American Music 251; Storyville SLP152
214   New Iberia Blues .... American Music Baby Dodds No. 4; Storyville SLP205
215   New Iberia Blues .... American Music 257; Storyville SLP152

Add Sidney "Jim Little" Brown (tu). Same personnel.
Recorded: New Orleans, August 1, 1944
385   I Love My Baby   Not issued
386   Honey Gal .... Not issued
387   Ballin' the Jack .... Not issued
388   Ballin' the Jack .... Not issued
389   Ballin' the Jack .... American Music LP643
390   Ballin' the Jack .... Not issued
391   Bugle Boy March .... Not issued
392   Bugle Boy March .... Not issued
393   Bugle Boy March   Not issued
394   How Long Blues .... Not issued
394½   How Long Blues .... Not issued
395   Muskrat Ramble .... Not issued
396   Careless Love .... Not issued
397   Careless Love .... Not issued
398   Careless Love .... Not issued
399   Blues .... Not issued

BUNK JOHNSON'S BAND

Bunk Johnson (tp), Jim Robinson (tb), George Lewis (cl), Lawrence Marrero (bj), Alcide "Slow Drag" Pavageau (b), Warren "Baby" Dodds (dr).
Recorded: New Orleans, August 2, 1944
401 When the Saints Go Marchin' In .... American Music LP638; Storyville SLP203
402 When the Saints Go Marchin' In .... American Music 252; Storyville SLP152
403 Ballin' the Jack .... American Music
404 Ballin' the Jack .... Storyville SLP205
405 High Society .... American Music Baby Dodds No. 4 (never issued)
406 Darktown Strutters' Ball .... Not issued
407 Darktown Strutters' Ball .... American Music 256; Storyville SLP152
408 Lord You're Good to Me .... Not issued
409 Lord You're Good to Me .... American Music LP647; Storyville SLP128
410 Careless Love .... Not issued
411 Careless Love .... American Music 258, LP647; Storyville SLP128
412 Panama .... Not issued
413 Panama .... Not issued
414 Panama .... American Music 255; Storyville SLP128
415 See See Rider .... American Music 251, LP638; Storyville SLP152
416 Blues .... American Music LP638; Storyville SLP205

Same personnel.
Recorded: New Orleans, August 3, 1944
501 Weary Blues .... Not issued
502 Weary Blues .... Not issued
503 Weary Blues .... Not issued
504 Clarinet Marmalade .... Not issued
505 Clarinet Marmalade .... Storyville SLP127
506 Yes, Yes, in Your Eyes .... American Music 253; Storyville SLP205
507 Royal Garden Blues .... Not issued
508 Royal Garden Blues .... Not issued
509 Streets of the City .... American Music LP647
510 Streets of the City .... American Music 256; Storyville SLP203, SLP128
511 Maryland, Maryland .... American Music Baby Dodds No. 3
512 Sister Kate .... Not issued
513 Sister Kate .... American Music 257; Storyville SLP128
514 Weary Blues .... American Music 258; Storyville SLP152
515 After You've Gone .... American Music LP647
516 Alabamy Bound .... Not issued
517 Alabamy Bound .... Storyville SLP205

Same personnel.
Recorded: New Orleans, August 4, 1944
601 Yes, Yes, in Your Eyes .... Not issued
602 Ole Miss .... Not issued
603 Ole Miss .... Not issued
604 Ole Miss .... Not issued
604½ You Are My Sunshine .... Not issued
605 When You Wore a Tulip .... American Music 255; Storyville SLP152
605½ Sugar Foot Stomp .... Rejected
606 Sugar Foot Stomp .... American Music LP643; Storyville SLP128
607 Sugar Foot Stomp .... Not issued
608 Tishomingo Blues .... Not issued
609 Tishomingo Blues .... Not issued
610 Darktown Strutters' Ball .... Not issued
611 Ballin' the Jack .... Not issued
612 Careless Love .... Not issued
613 Panama .... Not issued
614 Blues in C .... Not issued
615 Blues .... Not issued

BUNK JOHNSON'S STREET PARADERS
Bunk Johnson (tp), Jim Robinson (tb), George Lewis (cl), Lawrence Marrero (bj), Alcide "Slow Drag" Pavageau (b), Abbie "Kid Collins" Williams (dr).
Recorded: New Orleans, February 9, 1945
T-1   Tiger Rag .... Metronome B530; Esquire (English) 10-151, BSt 222; Riverside RLP12-119
T-2   Weary Blues .... Metronome B530; Esquire (English) 10-152, BSt 222; Riverside RLP12-119
T-3   Pallet on the Floor .... Metronome B531; Esquire (English) 10-151, BSt 230; Riverside SDP-11, RLP12-116
T-4   Careless Love .... Metronome B531; Esquire (English) 10-152, BSt 230; Riverside RLP12-119
        Sister Kate .... Not issued
     T-1 to T-4 are also issued on Riverside RLP1047; Esquire (English) EP181

BUNK JOHNSON - SIDNEY BECHET AND THEIR ORCHESTRA
Bunk Johnson (tp), Sandy Williams (tb), Sidney Bechet (cl), Cliff Jackson (p), George "Pops" Foster (b), Manzie Johnson (dr).
Recorded: New York City, March 10, 1945
BN223   Milenberg Joys .... Blue Note 564, BLP7008, BLP1201, BST 89902
        Basin Street Blues .... Not issued
BN225   Lord Let Me in the Lifeboat .... Blue Note BLP7008, BLP1202; Vogue (British) V2084
BN226   Days Beyond Recall .... Blue Note 564, BLP7008, BLP1201
        Porto Rico .... Not issued
BN228   Up in Sidney's Flat .... Blue Note BLP7008, BLP1202; Vogue (British) V2084

BUNK JOHNSON'S BAND
Bunk Johnson (tp), Jim Robinson (tb), George Lewis (cl), Lawrence Marrero (bj), Alcide "Slow Drag" Pavageau (b), Warren "Baby" Dodds (dr).
Recorded: New Orleans, May 14, 1945
822   Don't Fence Me In .... Rejected
823   Sister Kate .. Rejected
824   Sister Kate/Swanee River .. Rejected
825   Swanee River .... Storyville SLP202
826   Swanee River (drum solo) .... American Music Baby Dodds No. 1
827   Swanee River .... American Music Baby Dodds No. 1
828   Swanee River .... American Music 512
829   All the Whores Like the Way I Ride .... American Music LP644; Storyville SEP401
830   All the Whores Like the Way I Ride   Not issued
831   827 Blues .... American Music LP644; Storyville SEP401
832   827 Blues .... Not issued
833   827 Blues .... Not issued
834   Margie .... Not issued
835   Margie .. American Music 511
836   Runnin' Wild .... American Music 512; Storyville SLP202
837   You Always Hurt the One You Love .... American Music LP644; Storyville SEP401
838   I'm Making Believe .... Not issued
839   Amour   Not issued
840   The Sheik of Araby ... Storyville SLP202; Purist PU-7
(Only master 828 is used for American Music 512 — 825 is on some copies)

Same personnel. Warren "Baby" Dodds (vcl).
Recorded: New Orleans, May 15, 1945
841   Rum and Coca Cola .... Not issued
842   Carry Me Back to Old Virginia .... Not issued
843   Marie .... Not issued
844   Don't Fence Me In .... Not issued
845   Careless Love .... Not issued
846   Willie the Weeper .... Not issued
847   Listen to Me .... Not issued
848   Listen to Me .... Not issued
849   Listen to Me .... American Music 514; Baby Dodds No. 3
850   Sweet Georgia Brown   Not issued
851   High Society .... Not issued
852   High Society .... Not issued
853   Shine .... Not issued
854   Make Me a Pallet on the Floor .... Not issued
855   Slow Drag's Boogie Woogie .... Not issued
856   Slow Drag's Boogie Woogie .... Not issued
857   Slow Drag's Boogie Woogie .... Not issued
858   Make Me a Pallet on the Floor .... Not issued
859   Maria Elena .... Not issued
860   Maria Elena .... Not issued

Same personnel. Ed Johnson (vcl).
Recorded: New Orleans, May 17, 1945
864   Blues .... Rejected
865   Do Right Baby .... Not Issued
866   Do Right Baby .... American Music 511
867   Lonesome Road .... Not issued
868   Lonesome Road .... American Music LP638; Storyville SLP201
869   Golden Leaf Strut .... Not Issued
870   Golden Leaf Strut .... Not issued
871   Blues .... Rejected
872   My Old Kentucky Home .... Not issued
873   My Old Kentucky Home .. American Music 514; Storyville SLP202
874   Golden Leaf Strut .. American Music LP644; Storyville SEP401
887   Lady Be Good .... Purist PU-8
888   My Old Grey Bonnet .... Not issued
889   Ballin' the Jack .... Not issued
890   Indiana .... Not issued
891   The Waltz You Saved for Me .... Not issued
892   When You and I Were Young, Maggie .... Not issued

BUNK'S BRASS BAND
Bunk Johnson (tp), Kid Shots Madison (tp), Jim Robinson (tb), George Lewis (cl), Isadore Barbarin (ah), Adolphe Alexander (bh), Joe Clark (sou), Warren "Baby" Dodds (snare-dr), Lawrence Marrero (bass-dr).
Recorded: New Orleans, May 18, 1945
893   When the Saints Go Marching in .... Rejected
894   When the Saints Go Marching in .... American Music 102, LP643; Storyville SLP202; Dixie LP107

33

895 Just a Closer Walk with Thee .... Not issued
896 Just a Closer Walk with Thee .... American Music LP638; Storyville SLP202
897 Didn't He Ramble .... Not issued
898 Didn't He Ramble   American Music 103; Folkways FP57, FJ2803; Columbia C3L-30; Dixie LP107; Storyville SLP202; CBS BPG62234
899 Just a Little While .... Not issued
900 Just a Little While .... American Music 101, LP643; Dixie LP107; Storyville SLP202, SLP203
901 Nearer My God to Thee .... Not issued
902 Nearer My God to Thee .... American Music 102, Baby Dodds No. 1, LP643; Dixie LP107; Storyville SLP202
903 In Gloryland .... American Music 101, Baby Dodds No. 1; Dixie LP107; Storyville SLP202
904 St. Louis Blues .... Not issued
905 St. Louis Blues .... Not issued
906 Maryland, My Maryland . Not issued
907 Bye and Bye   American Music Baby Dodds No. 4
908 Maryland, My Maryland .... Not issued
909 Tell Me Your Dreams .... American Music 103, Baby Dodds No. 1; Dixie LP107; Storyville SLP202
910 Happy Birthday to You .... Not issued

BUNK JOHNSON AND HIS NEW ORLEANS BAND
Bunk Johnson (tp), Jim Robinson (tb), George Lewis (cl), Alton Purnell (p), Lawrence Marrero (bj), Alcide "Slow Drag" Pavageau (b), Warren "Baby" Dodds (dr).
Recorded: New York City, November 21, 1945
73149A Maryland, My Maryland .... Decca 25132
73149B Maryland, My Maryland .... Decca 25132; Vogue (British) V1036, Brunswick (British) OE9257; Ace of Hearts AH140; Brunswick (French/German) 10071EPB
73150A Alexander's Ragtime Band .... Decca 25132
73150B Alexander's Ragtime Band .... Decca 25132; Brunswick (British) 04437, OE9257; Ace of Hearts AH140; Brunswick (French/German) 10071EPB
73151A Tishomingo Blues   Decca 25131, DL8244; Brunswick (British) 04437, OE9257, LAT8124; Ace of Hearts AH140; Brunswick (French/German) 10071-EPB, 87003LPBM
73151B Tishomingo Blues .... Decca 25131
73152A You Always Hurt the One You Love .... Brunswick (British) OE9257; Brunswick (French/German) 10071EPB
73152B You Always Hurt the One You Love .... Decca 25131; Vogue (British) V1036; Ace of Hearts AH140

Same personnel.
Recorded: New York City, December 6, 1945
D5VB886-1 Sister Kate .... His Master's Voice (Australian) EA3438
D5VB886-2 Sister Kate .... Victor 40-0128; His Master's Voice B9517; RCA (German) EPA9696
D5VB887-1 Just a Closer Walk With Thee .... Victor 40-0127; His Master's Voice B9820
D5VB888-1 Snag It .... Victor 40-0126; His Master's Voice B9821; RCA (German) EPA9696
D5VB889-2 One Sweet Letter from You .... Victor 40-0129; His Master's Voice B9517

Same personnel.
Recorded: New York City, December 19, 1945
D5VB996-2   When the Saints Go Marching in .... Victor 40-0126, EPA35, LPT26, LPM(S)2982; His Master's Voice B9511, DLP1054; RCA (British) RD7713
D5VB997-1   High Society .... Victor 40-0127; His Master's Voice B9820
D5VB998-2   Darktown Strutters' Ball .... Victor 40-0128; His Master's Voice B9511; RCA (German) EPA9696
D5VB999-1   Franklin Street Blues .... Victor 40-0129; His Master's Voice B9821

Same personnel. Add Sister Ernestine B. Washington (vcl).
Recorded: New York City, January 2, 1946
D707   Does Jesus Care .... Jubilee 2501; Disc 6038; Asch AA-1 (alternate take); Mdsc (British) 1102
D708   The Lord Will Make a Way .... Jubilee 2501; Disc 6038; Mdsc (British) 1102
D709   Where Could I Go .... Jubilee 2502; Disc 6039; Asch AA-1; Mdsc (British) 1101
D710   God's Amazing Grace .... Jubilee 2502; Disc 6039; Mdsc (British) 1101
        The Jubilee titles were never issued. All four titles were also issued on Mdsc (British) EPM7-52.

WILLIE "BUNK" JOHNSON AND HIS NEW ORLEANS BAND
Bunk Johnson (tp), Jim Robinson (tb), George Lewis (cl), Alton Purnell (p), Lawrence Marrero (bj), Alcide "Slow Drag" Pavageau (b), Red Jones (dr).
Recorded: New York City, June 6, 1946
I Can't Escape from You .... V-Disc 630; Jay 6; Purist 1002
Snag It ....V-Disc 630; Jay 6; Purist 1002
Coquette .... Not issued
You Always Hurt the One You Love .... Not issued

BUNK JOHNSON
Bunk Johnson (tp), Don Ewell (p), Alphonse Steele (dr).
Recorded: New York City, April, 1946
929   In the Gloaming .... Not issued
930   In the Gloaming .... American Music 520, LP644; Storyville (Danish) SLP 202
931   I'll Take You Home Again, Kathleen .. American Music 520
932   You Got to See Mama Every Night .... American Music 519, LP644; Storyville (Danish) SLP202
933   Beautiful Doll .... American Music 519
934   When the Moon Comes Over the Mountain .... American Music 517
935   Where the River Shannon Flows .... American Music LP644
936   Where the River Shannon Flows .... American Music 517
937   Ja Da .... American Music 518, LP644; Storyville (Danish) SLP202
939   Poor Butterfly .... American Music 518

BUNK JOHNSON WITH DOC EVANS' BAND
Bunk Johnson (tp), Doc Evans (cnt), Dan Thompson (tb), Harry Blons (cl, ts), Don Ewell (p), Cliff Johnson (b), Warren Thewiss (dr).
Recorded: Minneapolis, May 3, 1947
Sister Kate (two takes) .... Unnumbered LP from Bunk Johnson Appreciation Society
High Society (two takes) .... Unnumbered LP from Bunk Johnson Appreciation Society
        On this session is also an interview between Bunk Johnson and Jack Stanley. It was recorded on May 2, 1947. Part of this interview is also on American Music LP643.

BUNK JOHNSON AND HIS BAND
Bunk Johnson (tp), Ed Cuffee (tb), Garvin Bushell (cl), Don Kirkpatrick (p), Danny Barker (g), Wellman Braud (b), Alphonse Steele (dr).
Recorded: New York City, December 23, 1947
151 The Entertainer .... Columbia GL520
152 The Minstrel Man .... Columbia GL520
153 Chloe .... Columbia GL520
154 Someday .... Columbia GL520

Same personnel.
Recorded: New York City, December 24, 1947
155 Hilarity Rag .... Columbia GL520
156 Kinklets .... Columbia GL520
157 You're Driving Me Crazy   Columbia GL520
158 Out of Nowhere .... Columbia GL520

Same personnel.
Recorded: New York City, December 26, 1947
159 That Teasin' Rag .... Columbia GL520
160 Some of These Days ... Columbia GL520
161 Till We Meet Again ... Columbia GL520
162 Maria Elena   Columbia GL520
   All selections from this session are also on Columbia (British) 33SX1015; Philips (British) BBL7231; Philips (German) B07009L.

ADDITIONS
BUNK JOHNSON'S STREET PARADERS
Recorded: New Orleans, February 9, 1945
T-4 Careless Love
T-2 Weary Blues
T-1 Tiger Rag
   Also issued on BYG 529.062.

BUNK JOHNSON AND HIS BAND
Recorded: Stuyvesant Casino, 140 Second Ave., New York City, August 11, 1947
   Issued on Nola LP3.

BUNK JOHNSON'S V-DISC VETERANS
Recorded: Los Angeles, July 11, 1944
Careless Love
I Ain't Gonna Give Nobody None of this Jelly Roll
Panama
Mama's Gone Goodbye

WILLIE "BUNK" JOHNSON AND HIS NEW ORLEANS BAND
Recorded: New York City, January 6, 1946
I Can't Escape From You
   Also issued on Jazz Trip 11.

BUNK JOHNSON'S STREET PARADERS
Recorded: New Orleans, February 9, 1945
T-4 Careless Love
T-2 Weary Blues
T-1 Tiger Rag
   Also issued on Joker SM3095. Note: Wrong date of recording printed on record jacket.

BUNK JOHNSON AND HIS NEW ORLEANS BAND
Recorded: New York City, January 6, 1946
I Can't Escape from You
Snag It

BUNK JOHNSON'S JAZZ BAND
Recorded: New Orleans, October 2, 1942
Big Chief Battle Axe
Franklin Street Blues

BUNK JOHNSON'S BAND
Recorded: New Orleans, May 14, 1945
Sheik of Araby

BUNK JOHNSON'S BAND
Recorded: New Orleans, May 17, 1945
Lady Be Good

BUNK JOHNSON'S V-DISC VETERANS
Recorded: Los Angeles, July 11, 1944
Mama's Gone Goodbye
Careless Love
Ain't Gonna' Give . . .
Panama
Lowdown Blues
Ballin' the Jack
Arkansas Blues
Spicy Advice
    Also issued on Nola LP6.

BUNK JOHNSON: A BRIEF CHRONOLOGY

1880 Born in New Orleans on December 27.

1894 Finished school (New Orleans University).

1894 Played with Adam Oliver's orchestra. First job as professional musician.

1895, 1896 With Buddy Bolden's band.

1898 With the Bob Russell Band.

1899 With various orchestras and brass bands in New Orleans.

1900 At Frankie Spano's Club with Jelly Roll Morton and Jim Parker. Also at Tom Anderson's with Mamie Desdoumes.

1901 On tour with the P. G. Loral Circus.

1903 In New York with McCabe's Minstrels.

1905 Played in Beaumont and traveled to Los Angeles, California.

1910 In New Orleans with Billy Marrero's Superior Orchestra.

1911 Left Superior Orchestra to join Frankie Dusen's Eagle Band.

1913 Left Dusen to work in the cabarets in the Red Light District. At Lala's on the corner of Liberty and Custom House with John Robichaux. Excursions with Jack Carey. A dance in New Iberia.

1914 Left New Orleans permanently. Taught in Mandeville for a year, managing the Fritz Family Orchestra; joined the orchestra at the Colonial Hotel in Bogalusa, Louisiana.

1916 With the Royal Orchestra in Lake Charles.

1917 With Walter Brundy in Baton Rouge.

1918 With the George Smart Set, a vaudeville-minstrel show.

1919 With the Vernon Brothers Circus.

1920s With Evan Thomas' Black Eagle Band in Crowley, and with Gus Fortinet's Banner Band in New Iberia. Usually he and Evan worked together for Fortinet.

1931 At the Yellow Front Cafe in Kansas City with Sammy Price, Julia Lee, and Baby Lovett.

1933 One night with Paul Barnes Band in Lake Charles.

1933-1937 With the W.P.A. Music Program in New Iberia as school teacher.

1937 Discovered by Frederic Ramsey, Jr. Included in *Jazzmen* book.

1937-1942 Worked in rice and sugar cane fields and at the Louisiana Hot Sauce plant.

1942 First recording session on June 11, in New Orleans. Second recording session on October 2, New Orleans.

1943 In San Francisco at the Museum of Art with Rudi Blesh and members of the Lu Watters' Yerba Buena Jazz Band. Recorded in San Francisco with Bertha Gonsoulin on April 11.

1944 Recorded with Yerba Buena Band in January and February. Recorded V-Disc Veterans session in Los Angeles on July 11. In New Orleans for recording with Lewis-Robinson band in July and August.

1945 At New Orleans Municipal Auditorium with Armstrong, Bechet, and J. C. Higgenbotham. Concert held on January 17. Recorded in New Orleans on February 9. In Boston with Sidney Bechet. Recorded with Bechet in New York on March 10, for Blue Note Records. Recorded in New Orleans on May 14, with Lewis-Robinson band. From September 28, 1945, to January 12, 1946, at the Stuyvesant Casino in New York with the Lewis-Robinson band. More recording sessions in New York on November 21 and December 19.

1946   With Ernestine Washington in New York for recording session on January 2. Last recording session with Lewis-Robinson band in New York on January 6. Trio recording date in April with Don Ewell and Alphonse Steele. From April 10 to May 31, in New York with band that included Don Ewell and Kaiser Marshall.

1947   Recorded in Minneapolis with Doc Evans in May. Dance dates in New York in November with a group of New York musicians. Last recording session in New York on December 23, 24, and 26.

1948   Back in New Iberia with the Banner Band. Suffered first stroke.

1949   Died in New Iberia on July 7.

STATE OF LOUISIANA
CERTIFICATE OF DEATH

BIRTH No. ___

STATE FILE No. **8 398**

1a. Last Name of Deceased	1b. First Name	1c. Second Name	2a. Month Day Year	2b. Hour
Johnson	Willie	"Bunk"	DATE OF DEATH: 7-7-49	1:35

3. Male or Female	4. Color or Race	5. Single, Married, Widowed, or Divorced	6a. Name of Husband or Wife	6b. Age
male	Negro	married	Maude Johnson	43

7. Date of Birth of Deceased	8. Age of Deceased	If under 1 day	9a. Birthplace (City or town)	9b. (State or Foreign Country)
2-27-1880	Years 63 Months 6 Days 10	Hours Min.	New Orleans	Louisiana

10a. Usual Occupation (Give kind of work done during most of working life, even if retired)	10b. Kind of Industry or Business	11. Was deceased ever in U.S. Armed Forces? (Yes, no, or unknown) (If yes, give war or dates of service)	
musician			

12a. City or Town—(If outside corporate limits write RURAL)	12b. Parish and Ward No.	12c. Length of Stay in this Place
New Iberia	Iberia	Life

12d. Name of Hospital or Institution (If not in hospital or institution give street address or location)		12e. Length of Stay in Hospital or Institution
Franklin		

13a. City or Town—(If outside corporate limits write RURAL)	13b. Parish and Ward No.	13c. State
New Iberia	Iberia	La

13d. Street Address—If rural give location	14. Citizen of what Country
Franklin St.	

15. Name of Father	15b. Birthplace of Father	16a. Maiden Name of Mother	16b. Birthplace of Mother
William Johnson	New Orleans	Theresa Jefferson	New Orleans

I certify that the above stated information is true and correct to the best of my knowledge.

17a. Signature of Informant	17b. Date of Signature
Maude Johnson	7-7-49

Interval Between Onset and Death

18. Disease or Condition Directly Leading to Death* (a) Cerebral hemorrhage

Antecedent Causes
Disease or conditions, if any, giving rise to the above cause (a) stating the underlying cause last.
Due to (b) Hypertension
Due to (c)

Other Significant Conditions
Conditions contributing to the death but not related to the disease or condition causing death.

19a. Date of Operation	19b. Major Findings of Operation	20. Autopsy Yes ☐ No ☐

21a. Accident, Suicide, or Homicide (Specify)	21b. Place of Injury (e.g., in or about home, farm, factory, street, office bldg., etc.)	21c. City, Town, or Ward No.	Parish	State

22. Time of Injury (Month) (Day) (Year) (Hour)	21e. Injury Occurred While at Work ☐ Not While at Work ☐	21f. How did injury occur?

I certify that I attended the deceased from 7-7-49 to 7-7-49 and that death occurred on the date and hour stated above.	23a. Signature of Physician	23b. Date of Signature
	R. J. St. Dix	7-8-49

24. Burial, Cremation, Removal 7-9-49	24a. Name of Cemetery or Crematory	24b. Location (City, Town, or Parish)	25. Signature of Funeral Director
	St. Edwards	New Iberia	Wilbert Fletcher

26. Burial Transit Permit Number 8452	27. Parish of Issue Iberia	28. Date of Issue 7-8-49	29. Signature of Local Registrar M. J. Martin

LOUISIANA STATE DEPARTMENT OF HEALTH, DIVISION OF PUBLIC HEALTH STATISTICS

JUL 21 1949

I CERTIFY THAT THE ABOVE IS A TRUE AND CORRECT COPY OF
A CERTIFICATE DULY REGISTERED WITH THE LOUISIANA STATE
DEPARTMENT OF HEALTH, BUREAU OF VITAL STATISTICS.

Andrew Hedmeg MD   _Anthony Graccio_

ACTING STATE HEALTH OFFICER   STATE REGISTRAR

JUN 25 1971

Certificate of death.

The Black Eagles Band in Crowley, Louisiana, about 1924. Left to right: Abraham Martin, Minor Decou, Lawrence Duhe, Robert Goby, Walter Thomas, Joe Avery, Evan Thomas.

Hypolite Potier, about 1913.

(Courtesy Harold Potier)

The Banner Band, with Bunk, Evan Thomas and Lawrence Duhé.

John Sanders, November, 1926.   (Courtesy John Sanders)

Lila Dusen, piano player and wife of Frank Dusen.

Theophile Thibodeaux at his home in Parks, Louisiana, 1974. (From the A. M. Sonnier collection)

Harold Potier at his home, 1974.   (From the A. M. Sonnier collection)

Center photo shows Joe Tilman from Thibodeaux, Louisiana, on tenor saxophone, and Gus "Bubba" Fortinet, Jr., on alto saxophone, with the Guitar Slim Band. Bubba is the son of Banner Band Leader Gus Fortinet. (Courtesy Harold Potier)

Hypolite "Iron Man" Potier played trumpet in the Banner Band before Bunk settled in New Iberia. (Courtesy Harold Potier)

Trumpeter Harold Potier was a close friend of Bunk's. (Courtesy Harold Potier)

Drummer and bassist John Sanders at 84, at his home in Jeanerette, Louisiana. (From the A. M. Sonnier collection)

Saxophone player and singer Chester Richardson in New Iberia. (From the A. M. Sonnier collection)

Wilfred Bocage. (Courtesy Harold Potier)

Beauragard Adam at his home in Cade, Louisiana, 1974. (From the **A. M. Sonnier** collection)

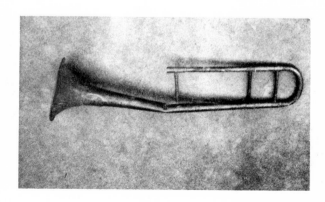

What is left of Gus Fortinet's trombone. Now in the possession of **Mercedes Potier.**

John Batice Brown's Dusky Stevedores Orchestra in the early 1920s. Brown is at the piano.

Drummer John Sanders and Harold Potier in 1974. (From the A. M. Sonnier collection)

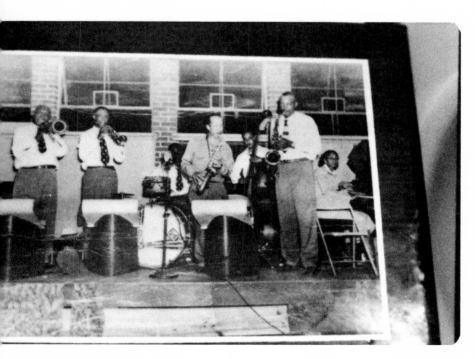

The Banner Band during its last years. Gus Fortinet (trombone), Harold Potier (trumpet), Louis Landry (bass), Beauragard Adam (alto sax), Mercedes Potier (piano).
(Courtesy Harold Potier)

WALTER "FATS" PICHON
APPEARING NIGHTLY-Piano Vocals at their BEST

Walter "Fats" Pichon. He and Bat Brown worked as a duo at the Pelican Club in New Orleans in 1920. (Courtesy Anthony Brown)

Duke Ellington and Billy Strayhorn at the White Eagle Club in Opelousas, Louisiana, in the 1940s. (Courtesy William M. Dauphin)

The Bat Brown Band in El Paso, Texas, in 1953. (Courtesy Anthony Brown)

PART TWO

RAMBLE ALL AROUND
IN AND OUT OF TOWN —

During the years between 1914 and 1949, except for a five-year span (1942-47) of recording and playing dates in New York and California, Bunk worked entirely in rural areas that spanned from Jeanerette, Louisiana, to Beaumont, Texas. His home was in New Iberia at this time. He had married, was buying property, and had established himself as a top-of-the-list professional in the field of music. The most influential orchestras in the area employed him regularly. He not only played trumpet, but was also proficient on tenor sax and tuba; the latter almost becoming his principal instrument when his teeth were bad. It would be safe to say that the first seventeen years, when he was away from New Orleans, were his most productive and personally rewarding period in his life. He performed with musicians of widely diverse talents and was by no means restricted to any one type or style of music. His association with the Banner Band kept him close to the framework of what was happening musically in New Orleans. Evan Thomas' Black Eagle Band afforded him the opportunity to expand the blues for as long as he desired. And Professor Oger's concert orchestra plunged him deeply into the classics. On those occasions when he felt the need to front his own band, Bunk had no trouble finding the type of musician who was sympathetic to his style of playing. There were many excellent musicians from which to choose. This undoubtedly was the primary reason why Bunk did not return to New Orleans for such a long time.

The lowlands, in the north and southwest areas of New Orleans, have for years been the spawning grounds for some of the most innovative musicians that that Mother City has ever embraced. Most of these men came to New Orleans when their careers were well along, and went on to make names for themselves in the annals of jazz history. Others stayed only a short time in the city, returning home to continue playing music and to live the slow pace of small town life. An example is Lawrence Duhé, who played in New Orleans and Chicago before moving to Lafayette, Louisiana. George Lewis made frequent trips outside of the city to work. At one point he was employed steadily by Evan Thomas. Yet the majority, including Beauragard Adam, Gus Fortinet, Evan Thomas,

Harold Potier and others, chose not to live in the city at all. In a way this tendency to avoid the big city was detrimental to their careers. Had they become involved in the evolution of early New Orleans jazz, they could have become famous in jazz history.

As in most rural areas, personal relationships are more valuable than gold. There are few instances of merely casual acquaintances. Country folk generally bind themselves with a more aggressive loyalty than inhabitants of a large city. This loyalty, each to the other, formed a bedrock that was the foundation for some of the most enduring bands and orchestras in jazz history. In addition to being the cause of a tightly bound musical family, that loyalty granted a trust which promoted an atmosphere responsible for the entire oral tradition in American folklore.

Cornetist Hypolite Charles studied with his father who was musically involved in Parks, Louisiana, at the time Buddy Bolden was playing "jass" in New Orleans. When young Charles went to the city at seventeen he found the music to be not unlike that which he played in his hometown. Harold Potier is still able to play melodies that are melodically, harmonically, and rhythmically close to some of the more popular New Orleans tunes played by his father, Hypolite Potier, at the turn of the century. Time and money, Bolden's worst enemies, did not permit him to travel far from his home in New Orleans. It does not seem possible that he was responsible for this birth and evolution of jazz that took place so far from the city. Bolden, like Hypolite Potier and August Charles, acquired his musical knowledge from slave parents and elders.

Bunk, George Lewis, and other New Orleans musicians like Mutt Carey and Buddy Petit, were aware of these resources that the lowlands had to offer. They constantly "fished" these areas for talent. It was a known fact that these country musicians were concerned more with improvisations than with score reading. Their aim was to reach the emotions of the audience by the extension of their own emotions. This could only be realized by the employment of spontaneous variations on simple material (the blues, spirituals, etc.). By insisting on freedom from the restrictions of musical notations, highly complicated rhythms of African origin were retained, altered slightly, and used as the basic, identifying factor of jazz music. Bunk preferred to play with Bolden because Bolden's band did not read. Hypolite Charles chose to work with Papa Celestin because he, too, was not hampered by a score. Buddy Petit not only could not read music, he was hesitant to hire sidemen who could. The list is endless. For every reading musician there were three others who either ignored the written note or chose from the beginning to play only by "air".

Another important factor in the progress of jazz outside the city of

New Orleans was the abundance of dance halls, cabarets, chicken shacks, honky-tonks, and ballrooms that were available to anyone with money. They required the same type of music as that played in the "fun" places of the Red Light District. Weekends were times for "unwinding." Field-hands, construction workers, small-time pimps and gamblers all gathered at these places for entertainment. They demanded that the music be loud, exuberant, and down to earth. The owners were more than willing to pay for the entertainment that attracted customers, and the amount of available work enticed more musicians to become involved in jazz music. Harold Potier recalls: "Musicians back then were good livers. The only way a man with no education could make it was to work hard in the fields. They would only get paid around a dollar seventy-five or two dollars a day. A fellow playing music could make as much as six dollars a night. That was a lot of money. You could live high on that for a couple of weeks."

Following is a list of bands and orchestras that functioned successfully in the jazz idiom in and around the town of New Iberia in the years between 1900 and 1930. Because there were so many orchestras and bands in New Orleans during these years, only the best survived to be documented here:

BANNER BAND   (New Iberia, Louisiana) 1920
    August Fortinet, trombone (leader)
    Robert Stafford, drums
    Jimmy Adam, clarinet
    Landers Roy, banjo
    Edwin Redium, violin
    Tom Avery, saxophone and bass
    Hypolite Potier, cornet
    Bunk Johnson, trumpet

HYPOLITE CHARLES' PARADE AND DANCE BAND (Parks, Louisiana) 1909
    Hypolite Charles, cornet
    Theophile Thibodeaux, cornet
    Hypolite Potier, cornet
    Simon Thibodeaux, trombone
    August Charles, baritone horn
    Gabriel Ledet, bass

THE STEVE ADAM TRIO (Jeanerette, Louisiana) 1918
    Steve Adam, guitar
    "Red", violin
    "Chup" Edwards, bass

THE BLACK EAGLE BAND (Crowley, Louisiana) 1925
    Evan Thomas, trumpet (leader)
    Lawrence Duhé, clarinet
    Robert Goby, saxophone
    Joe Avery, trombone
    Abraham Martin, banjo
    Walter Thomas, drums
    Minor Decou, bass
    Bunk Johnson, trumpet (in 1932)
    George Lewis, clarinet (in 1932)

ADAM FAMILY BAND (New Iberia, Louisiana) 1913
    Jimmy Adam, clarinet
    Beauragard Adam, trumpet
    Gertrude Adam, piano
    Melba Adam, piano, vocals
    Janus Adam, drums

ROYAL ORCHESTRA (Lake Charles, Louisiana) 1912
    Lyles Johnson, trombone
    "Monk", trumpet
    Doc Alphonse, guitar
    Paul, violin
    Lonzo, bass
    John Sanders, drums

WASHINGTON BAND (Cade, Louisiana) 1920
    Alfraze Washington, trumpet
    Hamilton Washington, trombone, banjo
    Carlton Wilson, bass, saxophone
    Harold Potier, trumpet
    Warnest Dequir, drums
    Bernard Durea, vocals

BROOKLYN FOUR QUARTET (New Iberia, Louisiana) 1921
      Chester J. Richardson
      Junious Nelson
      Alfred Grey   all vocals
      Eldridge Butler

VITALE BAND (Loreauville, Louisiana) 1905
      Jules Day, trumpet
      Tom Vital, trumpet
      Louis Vital, trombone
      August Charles, baritone horn
      George Adam, drums
      Pierre Vital, bass

YELPIN HOUNDS (Crowley, Louisiana) 1925
      Jules Babin, trumpet, trombone
      Harold Potier, trumpet
      "Tenance", c melody saxophone
      Quintard Miller, violin
      Son Adam, violin, guitar
      Sonny Hebert, bass

THE DUHE BROTHERS BAND (Laplace, Louisiana) 1914
      Lawrence Duhé, clarinet
      Dedana Duhé, violin, trombone
      B. L. Duhé, guitar
      Gaston Duhé, bass

IMPERIAL ORCHESTRA (Lake Charles, Louisiana) 1910
      Skinner Lutcher, guitar, bass
      Tony Babin, trombone
      Joe Babin, trumpet
      Allan Pratt, vocals
      John Sanders, drums

UNITED BRASS BAND (Parks, Louisiana) 1902
      George Potier, trumpet or cornet
      Hypolite Charles, cornet
      Theophile Thibodeaux, trumpet or cornet
      Simon Thibodeaux, trombone
      Amerson Washington, trombone
      Auguste Charles, baritone
      Buchanan Ledet, drums

BLACK DIAMOND BAND (Parks, Louisiana) 1922
  Theophile Thibodeaux, trumpet
  Alfraze Washington, trumpet
  Morris Dauphine, alto saxophone
  Simon Thibodeaux, trombone
  George Thomas, guitar
  Clay Deroussell, bass
  Buchanan Ledet, drums
  Garland Stewart, vocals

THE MARTEL FAMILY BAND (Opelousas, Louisiana) 1920
  Bert Martel, trumpet
  Dayton Martel, trumpet, trombone
  Hillery Martel, violin
  Willie Martel, banjo
  Joe Darensbourg, clarinet
  Various bass and drum players

DON FELTON BAND (Opelousas, Louisiana) 1925
  Bert Martel, trumpet
  Claxton Norman, trumpet
  Bradford Gordon, violin
  Miller Guidry
  Lawrence Henderson
  Sharlet Lemelle, piano
  Don Felton, drums
  Mary Bernard, vocals

SHORT BIOGRAPHICAL SKETCHES

ADAM, BEAURAGARD   (violin, trumpet, saxophone)
Born: April 6, 1897; New Iberia, Louisiana
Studied trumpet with his father, George W. Adam, for nine years before entering music professionally. Played in parade bands in Cade, St. Martinville, and New Iberia until 1918 when he joined the Banner Band. He was the driving force with this group until the early part of 1920. In June, 1920, he left New Iberia to attend medical college in New Orleans. While in New Orleans he studied music with Professor J. W. Nickerson. He later worked with Papa Celestin playing clarinet and saxophone at the Gypsy Tavern, The 45, and Tom Anderson's. He also worked in Napoleonville with Kid Rene and Clayborn Williams and with Zikka Mac in Lorgan City. Due to a number of misfortunes and the advent of World War I he was unable to complete his studies and had to drop out of school after only one year. After completing his military duties he returned to New Iberia and the Banner Band in November, 1923. In 1924 he moved to Crowley to play with the Black Eagles Band and with the Yelpin' Hounds with Jules Babin on trumpet and trombone. Played violin with Billy Mack's Merry Makers in New York in 1927. From 1927 to 1930 he traveled with minstrel shows. In the early 1930s he led his own band which included Frank Brown and Lawrence Duhé. Retired from music in the early 1940s because of illness.

ADAM, GEORGE W.   (drums)
Born: 1870; Cade, Louisiana
Died: 1930; Cade, Louisiana
Played drums in the Vital Band of Loreauville and Hypolite Charles' band in Parks. He was once the leader of a family band that included his children (Gertrude, piano; Melba, vocalist and piano; Jimmy, clarinet; Beauragard, trumpet; and Janus, drums). Most of his life was spent teaching school and playing in various area bands.

ADAM, JANUS   (drums)
Born: 1905; Cade, Louisiana
Died: 1972
Son of George W. Adam. Studied drums with his father. Worked with the Banner Band and the Jenkins Band in the late 1920s. Retired from music after his graduation from Southern University to become a teacher of industrial arts.

ADAM, JIMMY   (clarinet)
Born: 1900; New Iberia, Louisiana
Studied clarinet and music theory with his father, George W. Adam. Joined the Banner Band in 1920 and remained with that group for almost twenty years. One of their regular jobs was at Peron's Dance Hall in Youngville, which lasted over twenty years. In addition to this, Jimmy also functioned as a music teacher in the New Iberia Public School System and gave private lessons in his home. He ventured to New Orleans for a few months in 1922 to work with his brother, Beauragard Adam. Retired from music in the late 1940s. Now lives in Galveston, Texas.

ADAM, SON   (violin, guitar)
Born: 1890; New Iberia, Louisiana
Died: 1947; New Orleans, Louisiana
Started Beauragard Adam on violin. He and a saxophone player named "Tenance" played duets at the Big Apple and other New Iberia honky-tonks about 1907. Regular member of the Banner Band from 1910 to 1915. With the Yelpin' Hounds and the Jenkins Band from 1916 to 1920. Moved to New Orleans in the 1930s but did not play there.

ADAM, STEVE   (guitar)
Lived all his life in Jeanerette, Louisiana. Was a heavy drinker. Played in the John Daniel Orchestra in New Iberia and Franklin. Also with the Pallet Brothers Band. He did most of his professional playing with a trio that included "Red" on violin and "Chip" Edward on bass.

AVERY, JOSEPH "KID"   (trombone)
Born: October 3, 1892; Waggeman, Louisiana
Died: December 9, 1955; Waggeman, Louisiana
Avery studied with Dave Perkins from 1912 to 1915. Played with the Tulane Orchestra about 1922. Replaced Bob Thomas in Evan Thomas' Black Eagles Band in 1925. Toured with the Yelpin' Hounds Band. Leader of his own band from the early 1940s to the mid-1950s. He recorded for Southland Records in 1954. He also played with the Young Tuxedo Brass Band until World War II. In the fall of 1955 he became ill and died on December 9. His funeral was one of the largest held outside of New Orleans.

BANKS, JOE   (cornet)
Born: about 1882; Thibodeaux, Louisiana
Died: 1930; Thibodeaux, Louisiana
Banks played his first jobs with the Youka Brass Band in the early 1900s. He worked with the Youka and various other groups in Thibo-

deaux until the mid-1920s, helping many outstanding jazzmen by providing work for them. Banks left Thibodeaux in the late 1920s and moved to New Iberia so that he could play in the Banner Band. He remained with this group until his retirement.

BRAZLEE, HARRISON (trombone)
Born: October 25, 1888; New Orleans, Louisiana
Died: November, 1954
Brazlee began playing professionally with the Excelsior Brass Band of Mobile, Alabama, during the First World War. The Excelsior played most of the social affairs in Mobile until the first New Orleans jazz bands started playing at the Gomez Auditorium. In 1921 Brazlee left Mobile to join the Lena Orchestra in Jackson, Mississippi. From there he went to Beaumont, Texas, to play with Professor O'Shay. He toured with the Rabbit's Foot Minstrels, and then with Ringling Brothers Circus. When Joe Avery left the Black Eagles Band, Brazlee replaced him. He had to learn to improvise to stay with the band. In New Orleans, he played with trumpeter Dee Pierce at Luthjen's in the 1950s.

BROWN, JOHN BATICE (trumpet, alto and tenor sax)
Born: February 9, 1898; New Orleans, Louisiana
Died: December 15, 1968; El Paso, Texas
Studied with Henry "Red" Allen in New Orleans. Played in Allen's orchestra in his early twenties. Worked at the Pelican Club as a duo with Walter "Fats" Pichon for a number of years in the mid-1920s. Moved from New Orleans to Lafayette and then to El Paso in the early 1930s. Formed the famous Versatile Dusky Stevedores Orchestra in 1932. Active in music until his death.

BROWN, FRANK (trumpet)
Born: Broussard, Louisiana
Died: 1947; Lafayette, Louisiana
Played in Beauragard Adam's band for about three years in the early 1920s. Close friends of Lawrence Duhé. Worked with the Jenkins Band and the Black Eagles in Lafayette for a number of years in the 1940s. Group included clarinetist Duhé and other former members of the Black Eagle Band. Was active until his death.

BRUNDY, WALTER (drums)
Born: 1883; New Orleans, Louisiana
Died: 1941; Natchez, Mississippi
Played with the Original Superior Orchestra from 1905 to 1914. With

John Robichaux in 1912. Formed and led his own dance band with the Banner Band in 1933. Died in an auto accident.

CHARLES, AUGUSTE (baritone horn)
Born: 1862; Parks, Louisiana
Father of trumpeter Hypolite Charles. He played in his son's band in Parks and with the Vitale Band of Loreauville. A self-taught musician.

CHARLES, HYPOLITE (cornet)
Born: April 18, 1891; Parks, Louisiana
The son of a school teacher, Charles was encouraged in his interest in music by his father, Auguste, and upon organizing his own band prior to going to New Orleans, his father joined him as a member. The other musicians in the band were: Theophile Thibodeaux, lead trumpet; Hypolite Potier, second trumpet; Simon Thibodeaux, trombone; and Gabriel Ledet, bass.

He also played with the Vitale Band in Loreauville, Louisiana, with Jules Day on trumpet; Tom Vitale, second trumpet; Louis Vitale, trombone; and Pierre Vitale on bass. Auguste Charles joined them on the baritone horn. In 1908 Charles moved to New Orleans to study music with Eugene Moret, the brother of George Moret, leader of the Excelsior Brass Band. Within a year he was working with Manuel Parez at a dance hall on Dauphine and Elysian Fields. In 1911 he joined the Silver Leaf Orchestra led by violinist Albert Baptiste. Sam Dutrey played clarinet; his brother, Honore, was on trombone; Philip Nickerson played guitar; Jimmy Johnson, who had been with Buddy Bolden for years, played bass; and Willie Carter played drums. They played at debutante balls and private parties along St. Charles Avenue. He also began playing parades, with the Excelsior Brass Band. While playing for funerals and parades, the band would march all over town in places where the ground was rough and rocky and bumpy. Once he stumbled over a rock in the French Quarter and fell, cutting his lip. After that he would not play in parades where music was read. He joined Papa Celestin's Tuxedo Brass Band and remained there a number of years.

He joined the Maple Leaf Orchestra in 1919 and opened with them at the Washington Youree Hotel in Shreveport in July of that year. They came back to New Orleans in the fall. A few months later, Charles organized his own orchestra and went to the Moulin Rouge. His group was composed of Sonny Henry, trombone; Joe Welch, drums; Sam Dutrey, clarinet; Emile Bigard, violin; and Camille Todd, piano. He studied with Camille Todd in 1909.

When the famed orchestra leader A. J. Piron toured New York a second time, Charles' orchestra replaced him at Tranchina's with only one change in personnel; Robert Hall replaced Dutrey on clarinet.

Charles gave up playing in 1925, when after performing for a Sunday afternoon tea dance, he suffered a ruptured spleen. He was confined to his bed for a year. He sold life insurance in New Orleans until 1940, when he then turned over his accounts to Peter Bocage and returned to Parks to take over his father's grocery store.

DARENSBOURG, JOE   (clarinet, tenor saxophone)
Born: July 9, 1906; Baton Rouge, Louisiana
Darensbourg started playing music on the violin and piano. He later received lessons on clarinet from Manuel Roque in Baton Rouge and Alphonse Picou in New Orleans. His professional career began in 1924 with the Martel Family Band in Opelousas. He was married to trumpeter Burt Martel's oldest sister. In the later 1920s he was associated with Fate Marable and Charlie Creath in St. Louis. He then played for about a year in Harrisburg, Illinois, where he was shot by gangsters. After his recovery he played with Jelly Roll Morton in Cairo, Illinois, and then traveled across country with the A. G. Barnes' Circus Band. During the 1920s he played aboard various passenger liners, and later led his own band in Vancouver and Seattle. The 1930s found him touring with the Vic Sewell Band and playing on the passenger boats to Alaska. In the 1940s he played with the Kid Ory Band in California. He also worked with pianist Johnny Wittwer and Doc Exner in Seattle, the Red Foxx Hungry Hounds, Joe Liggins and his Honey-drippers, and Wingy Manone. During the 1950s he played with Gene Mayl's Dixie Rhythm Kings in Ohio, and with Teddy Buckner. On his own he recorded "Yellow Dog Blues" which became the nation's overnight juke-box favorite. In 1961, he worked with John St. Cyr's Young Men of New Orleans, and then joined Louis Armstrong's All Stars from September, 1961 to June, 1964.

DAUPHINE, MORRIS   (clarinet, alto saxophone)
Born: 1906; Parks, Louisiana
Dauphine left Parks in 1920 to study at the Howard Institute in New Iberia. While there, he studied clarinet for five years with Jimmy Adams, a noted member of the Banner Band. In 1925, he moved to New Orleans to help his uncle who operated a drugstore on South Galvez Street. The intentions of his parents were for him to attend medical school. After much deliberation, he was allowed to try his hand at music. He took lessons with Lorenzo Tio, Jr., and soon joined Oscar Celestin's Tuxedo Band. He stayed with the Tuxedo Band for two years, playing in parades and dances.

In 1927, he journeyed to Baton Rouge to accept an offer to play with the Deluxe Harmony Players, the city's most popular dance band. They played benefit concerts and social events to raise funds for the refugees of the 1927 floods.

In 1930, on the advice of his physician, Dauphine stopped playing and returned to his native Parks. There, he opened a night club and operated it for ten years. During this period he played occasionally with various local bands including the Banner Band.

"I never did play with Bunk. You see, when I came back to New Iberia, I was playing very little music. I had this business and everything. I knew old Bunk well though. We used to talk a whole lot. He had a style of playing that was ahead of most of us. He knew so much about music. Bands in those days always played by music—you had to know how to read, even if it was just enough to fake it. Well, that Bunk could play all the parts on his cornet. He was like a king to the people around here. There was always a large crowd at the dances that he would play. When he died, people from all over came to pay their respects. Now hardly anybody knows where his grave is. I guess that's the way it is—when you're done. I never heard any of his records. They tell me he had made quite a few. He must have been famous before he died."

DUHE', LAWRENCE (clarinet)
Born: April 30, 1887; LaPlace, Louisiana
Died: 1960; Lafayette, Louisiana

Duhé's musical talent was inherited. He began playing jazz and the blues at a very early age in his hometown. His father, Evariste Duhé, worked at the LaPlace Sugar Refinery as a dryer and played violin in his own band as well as other bands in LaPlace. His sisters played organ and autoharp in church. The Duhé Brothers Band reigned in LaPlace. Gaston played bass violin; Blace, who was later to graduate from Harvard and practice medicine in Beaumont, Texas, played guitar; Dedana, the eldest, played trombone and violin; and Lawrence played guitar and clarinet. All of their music was performed by ear.

In 1901 Lawrence was sent to New Orleans to attend the third grade at Straight University. After finishing school he returned to LaPlace and took a job with the post office. In order to join a band led by trombonist Ed Ory he abandoned the guitar and began to concentrate on the clarinet. As a result, this was to become his only instrument.

In 1913 Ory took his group to New Orleans and defeated Bab Frank's band in a contest at Dixie Park. They decided to stay in New Orleans and used John Joseph's barber shop as their headquarters. This was a time of growth for Duhé. The qualities of leadership were taught to him by Ory and he took lessons from Lorenzo Tio, Jr., and George Baquet on the clarinet. His first venture as a leader was a job at the 101 Ranch which lasted only a few months. Band members were: Walter Decou, piano;

Johnny St. Cyr, guitar; Sidney Desvigne, cornet; and John Benoit, drums. Duhé managed to keep the band together and working for about a year in places like Pete Lala's and Tom Anderson's.

He went to Chicago in April, 1917. He was booked into the Delux Cafe, playing from 8 P.M. until midnight and then at the Royal Gardens, from 1 A.M to 4 A.M., seven days a week. "Sugar" Johnny Smith was on cornet; Roy Palmer, trombone; Louis Keppard, guitar; Fred "Bebe" Hall, drums; Wellman Brieux, bass; and Lil Hardin, whom he introduced to Louis Armstrong, was on piano. The great Bill Robinson danced in the floor show. When "Sugar" Johnny died of pneumonia in the winter of 1918, Mutt Carey replaced him. Mutt, however, could not take the cold weather and left the band without notice to return to New Orleans. There, he influenced Joe Oliver, who was leaving for Chicago for another job, to fill in the trumpet chair in the Duhé Band. Oliver joined Duhé at the Dreamland.

As time went on, trouble arose between Duhé, Oliver and Roy Palmer. Oliver insisted that Duhé fire Palmer for sleeping on the job. Duhé refused. Their differences remained until 1919, when Duhé and Palmer were left without a band. Before this, however, he had the honor of leading the first jazz band to play at a World Series game: the Cincinnati Red Sox versus the Chicago White Sox in 1919. Duhé played first clarinet. The other members of the band were: Jimmy Pallio, tenor saxophone; George Field, trombone; Joe Oliver, trumpet; Willie Humphrey, second clarinet; Emmett Scott, banjo; Wilmore Breaux, bass; and Minor Hall, drums.

In 1932 Duhé became ill from an ulcer that had been bothering him for some time. His doctor advised him to go to Arizona but he moved south to New Orleans instead. After a short while in the city, Jack Carey persuaded him to join the excursion circuit which toured from New Orleans to Lafayette. Duhé was happy to be playing music again and on his first trip to Lafayette, Evan Thomas, the legendary trumpet player from Crowley, met him at the train station with some members of his Black Eagles Band. He offered Duhé $35 a week plus room and board to work with him. Duhé accepted on the spot, and was rushed to Crowley with only his clarinet to play a dance that night. A young lady who ran the boarding house where he was to stay helped him get some clothes. He eventually married her and moved to Lafayette. His association with Evan Thomas lasted about ten years.

During this time he also worked with Gus Fortinet's Banner Band in New Iberia. Bunk Johnson, who was living in New Iberia at this time, played second trumpet with Fortinet. Together they traveled through northern Louisiana and Texas. After Evan was murdered at a dance in

Rayne, Louisiana, in 1932, Duhé went on the road with the Rabbit's Foot Minstrels and toured throughout the South.

Being away from his wife was not exactly an ideal situation for him, and after a few months he left the minstrels to join Frank Brown's band in Lafayette. Except for a week with Pinchback Touro's Lincoln Band at a fair in Morgan City, Louisiana, in the mid 1930s, Duhé played regularly with Brown at the Four Corners in Lafayette until 1945.

That year marked the end of his career as a professional musician. For some reason he lost interest in playing. He constantly refused jobs, including an offer from Kid Ory to join his band in California. He lived quietly with his memories; pictures of musicians he once worked with, his old clarinet, records, and other memorabilia that were collected during his life.

He had written three songs in the late 1920s that were recorded on the Cinerama Song Record Label. Available copies are hard to find. With the exception of these songs, no other recordings have been made.

Duhé died quietly at his home in Lafayette at the age of 73. He did not receive the traditional New Orleans funeral but most of the musicians that he was at one time associated were there. After services, his body was taken to Reserve, Louisiana, for burial.

DUSEN, LILA WILLIAMS (piano, vocalist)
Born: about 1889; New Iberia, Louisiana
Wife of trombone player Frank Dusen; an aunt of Gus Fortinet. Played piano for Sweet Papa Snowball in Galveston, Texas. Most of her career involved playing and singing in minstrels throughout the South. After retiring from music she became a successful dance hall operator.

DUTREY, SAM, JR. (clarinet)
Born: 1915; New Orleans, Louisiana
Dutrey was not as deeply involved in music as was his father. He was a top clarinet player but only played occasional parade and dance jobs. He worked with Joe Robichaux in the early 1930s, and then went to Crowley to play with Evan Thomas' Black Eagles. After leaving the Black Eagles, he returned to New Orleans. Dutrey recorded on the Southland Records label.

EVAN, ROY (drums)
Born: about 1890; Lafayette, Louisiana
Died: about 1943; Lafayette, Louisiana
Evan played drums on the famed "second session" of the Sam Morgan Band in the fall of 1927. He played with Earl Humphrey and Buddy

Petit in 1920. In 1927 he played with Henry "Red" Allen. He returned to Lafayette in the 1930s and worked occasionally with Frank Brown and Gus Fortinet. He recorded with Petit and with George Lewis and Lee Collins during 1924 session. The recording was not released. He replaced drummer "Shine" Williams in the Sam Morgan Band in 1927.

FORTINET, GUS   (trombone)
Born: December 15, 1888; New Iberia, Louisiana
Died: June 12, 1967; New Orleans, Louisiana
Gus started playing professionally in his early teens around New Iberia. He is the nephew of trombone player Frankie Dusen and his wife Lila, who was once a trouper with Sweet Papa Snowball in Beaumont, Texas. His sister, Annette, was a music teacher at St. Edward's Catholic Church in New Iberia.

Gus earned a large part of his income by working as a bartender and professional barber, a trade he learned from his father. He tended bar at the Hollywood Social Club and the Tech Bar in New Iberia. The Tech Bar was a gathering place for local musicians as well as transients like Louis Armstrong and Dinah Washington.

By 1925 the Banner Band was well established. Work was plentiful and only the best musicians worked with him. During his years as bandleader, Gus developed a distinctive sound on the trombone by welding three kazoo together and using them as a mute. He played forcefully and it is said that, at times, his method of choking with this mute would cause blisters to appear on his horn.

When he was in his early forties, Gus and his son, saxophonist Gus Junior, went on the road with "The Little Joe Band" from Alexandria, Louisiana. They traveled as far as New York City playing their brand of jazz music.

Fortinet remained active in music until the late 1950s when he became the victim of an illness that resulted in the amputation of both legs. He died at Charity Hospital in New Orleans on June 12, 1967 and was buried at St. Peter's Cemetery in New Iberia.

FOSTER, ABBIE "CHINEE"   (drums, vocal)
Born: March 19, 1900; New Orleans, Louisiana
Died: September 15, 1962
Foster was self-taught on the drums and played his first professional job at St. Catherine's Hall when he was ten years old. From 1916 to 1918 he played during the afternoon and evenings at the Iroquois Theatre with Jimmy Palao on violin and Margaret DeVerne on piano. He replaced Henry Zeno in the Tuxedo Orchestra in 1917, and was with that

group until the early 1930s. In 1922 he went to the Houston-Galveston area with Buddy Petit, and toured the South with Mack Thomas in 1923. He played occasional jobs with the Banner Band in the late 1920s. He recorded with Oscar Celestin in the spring of 1927. In 1930 Foster led his own band on the cruise ship, *S. S. Madison*. The name of his band was "Chinee's Crazy Kattes". The members included Buddy Petit, Israel Gorman, Fletcher Henderson, and it toured for three months. At the end of this period he was hospitalized, and became inactive until the early 1950s. He recorded for the Atlantic Records' "Jazz at Preservation Hall" series, and played drums with Billie and De De Pierce until his death in 1962.

GABRIEL, JOE (violin, mandolin)
Born: 1880; Thibodeaux, Louisiana
Joe Gabriel started his own band in Thibodeaux around 1900. In 1910, members of the band were: Willie James, cornet; Lewis James, clarinet; Neddy James, guitar; Albert Jiles, Sr., drums; and a man named Alfred on bass. In 1912 Adam Dunbar replaced Neddy James, and in 1913 Albert Jiles died and was replaced by his son. Gabriel played with the Youka Brass Band from 1910 to about 1920. During this time he played quite a few jobs with the Banner Band in New Iberia. He was one of the few violin players that Fortinet used during the early years. Gabriel led his band and played professionally until 1920, when he retired to become a grocer.

GOBY, ROBERT (tenor saxophone)
Died: 1926; Lafayette, Louisiana
Played mostly in minstrels and on tours. Freelanced with area bands in the early 1920s. Longest period of steady employment was with Evan Thomas' Black Eagles Band.

GORDON, BRADFORD (violin)
Born: about 1910; Opelousas, Louisiana
Played most of his professional career with the Martel Family Band and the Don Felton Band from Opelousas. After the Martel Band broke up, he freelanced with country bands until 1949 and then retired from music completely. He was highly regarded by his fellow musicians. He was referred to as one of the exceptionally gifted non-reading musicians.

HAMILTON, CHARLES (piano, banjo)
Born: April 28, 1904; Ama, Louisiana
Hamilton played his first professional jobs with Evan Thomas' Black

72

Eagles Band in 1927. After leaving the Black Eagles, he worked solo and with small area bands until he became part of the big dance band era. He was with Herb Leary's orchestra in the late 1920s and 1930s. During the 1960s he returned to traditional jazz. He toured the Orient with George Lewis' band and played frequently at Preservation Hall.

HAMILTON, GEORGE "POP"   (trumpet, alto horn, bass, tuba)
   Born: October 9, 1888; New Iberia, Louisiana
   Hamilton was leader of the short-lived Lions Brass Band in 1928. He organized his own band in 1930, which lasted only about a year before it was killed off by the Depression. In 1919 he was with Chris Kelly and then with Sam Morgan in the early 1920s. He was also a member of the early bands of Bunk Johnson, Evan Thomas and Lawrence Duhé, and worked with Gus Fortinet's Banner Band around 1909.

JAMES, LEWIS   (clarinet, saxophone, bass)
   Born: April 9, 1890; Thibodeaux, Louisiana
   Lewis James came from a musical family. His father played and so did his four brothers. He taught himself to play Joe Gabriel's violin when he was only twelve years old. At fifteen he began playing saxophone and clarinet. In 1917 he went to New Orleans and played jobs with Amos Riley, Frankie Dusen, and Jack Carey. He later got a regular job at Villa's Cabaret with Joe Howard on cornet and Manuel Manetta on piano. When the District closed, James began working as porter at the Whitney Bank and managed to play occasional jobs until 1920. He moved back to Thibodeaux that year and organized the James Brothers Orchestra. For the next six years he played in and around Thibodeaux and also for a time with the Banner Band in New Iberia. He moved back to New Orleans in 1926 and began playing with Louis Dumaine. They recorded in 1927. James stayed with Dumaine until the early years of the Depression, when he was replaced by Israel Gorman. He returned a few years later and remained with Dumaine (playing bass) until 1949. In the 1950s he played bass for Percy Humphrey and was still seen occasionally at Preservation Hall in 1965.

LANDRY, LEWIS   (bass)
   Born: September 9, 1921; Lake Charles, Louisiana
   Studied music with his father and "Skinner" Lutcher in Lake Charles. Played his first professional jobs with the Imperial Orchestra and the Royal Orchestra in Lake Charles. Moved to New Iberia in 1941. Started playing with the Banner Band in that year and remained with them for

about ten years. Worked occasional jobs with Bunk around New Iberia. Active with many area bands until his retirement in the mid 1960s.

LEDET, GABRIEL (bass)
Born: 1890; Parks, Louisiana
A very strong and musical bass player. Worked mostly in the bands of Hypolite Charles and the Thibodeaux Brothers. Played with the Banner Band in its earliest years. Active in music until around 1929.

MARTIN, ABRAHAM (banjo)
Born: Rayne, Louisiana
Regular member of the Black Eagle Band in the 1920s. Played with the Banner Band, usually as a replacement.

MILLIAN, BAKER (tenor saxophone)
Born: 1908; Crowley, Louisiana
Millian started with the piano, then switched to alto and "C" melody saxes before deciding on the tenor sax. His first professional work was with the Yelpin' Hounds Band in Crowley. He left the Yelpin' Hounds in the mid-1920s to play, briefly, with Chris Kelly in New Orleans. He later joined the Black Eagles Band from 1927 to 1929. He moved to Texas in 1929 and played with the Buffalo Rhythm Stompers before joining Giles Mitchell's band in Houston in 1931. He joined Chester Boone's band at the Harlem Grill in Houston the following year. From 1933 to 1938 he was the featured tenor sax soloist with Boots and His Buddies, led by drummer Clifford "Boots" Douglas. In 1943 he played occasional jobs with his old friend, Bunk. He moved to California in the 1940s and continued to play throughout the 1950s and 1960s, mostly around San Francisco and Oakland.

OLIVER, MARY ELLA FORTINET (piano)
Born: New Iberia, Louisiana
Daughter of Gus Fortinet. She was a music teacher and played in the Banner Band only when her sister, Mercedes, could not play. She was a very good reader and occasionally played from a violin part. She was able to improvise, and the blues was her favorite music.

POTIER, HAROLD (trumpet)
Born: 1911; Parks, Louisiana
Harold's father, Hypolite Potier, taught him to be a trumpet player in the Banner Band. When he was twelve years old, be began his studies on trumpet, clarinet, and saxophone at the Oger School of Music in

Crowley, Louisiana. Professor Oger was a graduate of the Mozart Conservatory of Music, and before his health failed him, he toured with the Paris Symphony, the largest orchestra in the world at that time.

"When he took sick and had to leave the orchestra, he was in Alexandria, Egypt," Potier recalls. "The professor returned to his home in Crowley to teach music. He was well known and well respected by both jazz and classical musicians. When people like Bunk would get into arguments about music, they would go to the professor to settle their disputes."

Potier started playing with the Banner Band when he was out of school. During World War II, he served in the army playing trumpet with the 418th Armed Forces Band. Harold Baker of the Duke Ellington Orchestra was in the same band. They toured throughout the world.

After the war, he returned to New Iberia where he played with the Banner Band, the Black Eagles Band, the Yelpin' Hounds, and the Jenkins Band. He also worked, on one occasion, with "Sweet Emma" Barrett.

When he was 19 years old, he was offered jobs with Fletcher Henderson and Earl Hines. He had just married and turned down the offers in order to stay in New Iberia with his wife, Mercedes Fortinet, and work with the local bands.

He composed and arranged tunes for the Banner Band, but they were never recorded.

No longer active as a musician, Potier now makes woodcarving his profession.

POTIER, HYPOLITE (cornet)
Born: about 1890; Parks, Louisiana

Father of trumpeter Harold Potier. Cornetist in Hypolite Charles' band in Parks around 1905. Other members of this band were: Theophile Thibodeaux, trumpet; Simon Thibodeaux, trombone; Gabriel Ledet, bass; and Auguste Charles, baritone horn.

According to Harold Potier, the nickname "Iron Man" was given to him when he played with the marching bands. He was the only man strong enough to march and play all day without getting tired.

He was a regular with the Banner Band from the beginning. Most trumpet players in the area could not compete with Potier's robust trombone style. When he stopped playing in the late twenties, Bunk and Evan Thomas filled his position.

POTIER, MERCEDES (piano)
Daughter of Gus Fortinet. Mercedes played piano in her father's band until it ceased to operate.

She received her musical training from Xavier University in New Orleans and the University of Southwestern Louisiana. After leaving school and returning to New Iberia, she became involved in music as a profession.

Although most of her playing was done in the Banner Band, she did work with the Black Eagles and the Yelpin' Hounds. Her association with Bunk was very close. They played together when he was with the Banner Band.

Mercedes recalls: "Bunk was a funny person. He was drinking a whole lot during the time we played together. That could be why he had such a sense of humor. No matter how serious the situation was, Bunk would find something funny to say. Really knew how to keep everybody from getting in the dumps. He was one of the best trumpet players that I ever heard. Knew his music. He had to to get along with me!

"There is one thing about Bunk that few people in the big cities know. They don't know about him playing the tuba. He did not stop playing music when his teeth went bad. I don't remember Bunk ever leaving music. He had other jobs to make more money but he always played music. He would play the tuba in my father's band. Funny thing about that is, he would play like he was on his trumpet.

"One night at a dance in New Iberia, he was drunk and he told me that he was going to lay on the floor and play the tuba the same way Louis (Armstrong) plays his trumpet. He got on the floor alright but he could not make a sound on his horn. Boy, he really tried though—just huffin' and puffin'. That was Bunk for you. Had a way with women too.

"Evan Thomas was something on trumpet. He could play real high and powerful like Louis Armstrong. He was a blues player, though. Bunk couldn't play high but his ideas and execution were more advanced than Evan's. That is why Bunk played second trumpet—he could fill in better. He played that way until the time he died. Always pretty. Too bad he wasn't a younger man when he started making records."

PRATT, ALLAN (vocals)
Born: New Iberia, Louisiana
Vocalist with the Banner Band around 1927. Became chauffeur and booking-agent for the Banner Band after his retirement.

REDIUM, ED (violin, banjo)
Born: 1878; Cade, Louisiana
Died: 1939; Cade, Louisiana
Studied violin with George Adam. Mostly self-taught on banjo. Became proficient enough to become musical director for the Banner Band until

1930. Worked on excursions from Lake Charles to New Orleans during the 1930s. Also played in a number of minstrel shows around Lafayette. Had replacement jobs with the Washington Band and Adam Jenkin's Band during most of his musical career. Like many musicians in this area, Redium had to rely on work in the rice and sugar cane fields to support his family. Was active in music until his death.

RICHARDSON, CHESTER J. (saxophone, vocal)
Born: December 29, 1908; New Iberia, Louisiana
Richardson began playing saxophone with the Banner Band in his early twenties. He could not read music well enough to continue so he tried singing. As a result, he became the band's regular vocalist. He moved to Galveston, Texas, in 1932 and played with a number of bands until 1935. Upon his return to New Iberia, he rejoined the Banner Band and also sang with the vocal group, The Brooklyn Four Quartet. Other members were: Junious Nelson, Alfred Grey, and Eldridge Butler.
"People say a lot of things about Bunk. All I know is that he was a good musician. He could play *anything*. Every time we had a rehearsal Bunk would come in late and almost drunk. That wouldn't bother us none though. He was always able to fall right in with the music. He really enjoyed himself that way."

SAUNDERS, JOHN (drums, bass)
Born: August, 1890; Berwick, Louisiana
Started playing at the age of 12. Worked with trumpeter John Daniel's orchestra in 1908, and with singer Zicca Mac in 1912. Moved to Lake Charles in 1914 and played with the Royal Orchestra. He learned to play bass while in Lake Charles and doubled on that instrument and drums in both the Royal and Imperial Orchestras. In 1920 he moved to New Iberia and became a member of the original Banner Band. Was with Banner when they played opposite Count Basie in Galveston, Texas, in the early 1930s. Off and on with the Banner Band and the John Daniel Orchestra until around 1940.

THIBODEAUX, SIMON (trombone)
Born: April 12, 1889; Parks, Louisiana
Studied music with Peter Carey. Played professionally for about 35 years in the Parks area. Played in the United Brass Band and the Black Diamond Band. His remaining years of musical endeavor were with the Thibodeaux Band, a group he co-led with his brother, Theophile.

THIBODEAUX, THEOPHILE (trumpet)
Born: December 16, 1890; Parks, Louisiana
Studied music with Peter Carey. First professional job with Peter Carey's orchestra when he was so small he had to stand on a chair to be seen. Joined the United Brass Band in 1920 and played with this group for twenty years. In 1940 Theophile joined the Black Diamond Band. Members included: Simon Thibodeaux, trombone; George Thomas, guitar; John Gerrard, trumpet; Morris Dauphine, saxophone; Alphonse Washington, trumpet; Buchanan Ledet, drums; Clay Derussell, bass; and Garland Stewart, vocals. During this time he played parades for the Masons and the Y.M.P.B.A. With the Washington Band in 1945 until his retirement in 1952.

THOMAS, BOB (trombone)
Born: about 1898; New Orleans, Louisiana
Died: 1960
Bob Thomas worked with Evan Thomas' (no relation) Black Eagles Band in the early 1920s, touring Louisiana and East Texas. He lived in New Iberia and worked with the Banner Band when not working for the Black Eagles Band. Thomas worked outside of New Orleans most of his life. He recorded and went on frequent tours with Paul Barbarin in the 1950s.

THOMAS, EVAN (trumpet)
Born: about 1890; Crowley, Louisiana
Died: 1932; Rayne, Louisiana
Leader of the Black Eagles Band. He played in the small towns west of New Orleans and Texas most of his life. He had a tremendous range and an intense, powerful style. Had a habit of advertising his dances by sitting in the show-window of a store and blowing his horn for the people. This was his way of "calling his children home". When work was slow, Evan played first trumpet in Gus Fortinet's society orchestra and the Banner Band. Bunk and George Lewis were with Evan in 1932, when he was murdered. A man named John Gilbey came up to the bandstand shouting that Evan was fooling with his wife. He pushed his way onto the bandstand and, in a frenzy of rage, fatally stabbed Evan after a short, vicious struggle. Evan stumbled through the crowd and reached the steps of a church across the street before he died.

THOMAS, GEORGE (banjo)
Died: 1928; Crowley, Louisiana
First cousin of Evan Thomas. Did not rely on music as his sole source of income. Played mostly with the Black Eagles and Jenkins Bands.

WILSON, CARLTON (saxophone, bass)
Born: 1910; Cade, Louisiana
Died: 1970; Cade, Louisiana
First lessons in music were on the "c" melody saxophone. He added the bass after he began to play professionally. Took over as leader of the Banner Band for a short period during World War II. Played with the Washington Band in Cade in 1927.

ZARDIS, CHESTER (bass)
Born: May 27, 1900; New Iberia, Louisiana
Zardis played bass with Buddy Petit's band in Mandeville, Louisiana, when he was around 14 years old. After Petit's band, he worked with Chris Kelly, Kid Bena, and Kid Howard. He worked with Sidney Desvigne in 1930-31, and in 1935 he had his own band at Mamie's Beer Garden. Members were Paul Barnes, George Williams Coo Coo Talbert, and Johnny St. Cyr. This group lasted until 1938. In 1942, he made recordings with Bunk Johnson and with the George Lewis Band in 1943. He became a regular performer at Preservation Hall in 1966. Zardis started playing bass in 1915. He took lessons from Dave Perkins and Billy Marrero, and then started playing with the Merit Band in 1919. Played with James Clayton and Evan Thomas in Crowley from 1932 to 1934. In 1936 and 1937, while with Duke Dejan's Dixie Rhythm Band, Zardis played for a short time in Count Basie's Band at the Apollo in New York. He worked with Walter Pichon on the cruise ship, *S. S. Capitol,* in 1939, and then rejoined Kid Clayton in 1940. After serving in the Army during World War II he played with Floyd Hunt and George Morrison in Denver, Colorado, and Henry Lowe in Philadelphia. He left music in 1954 to farm in New Iberia. His retirement was short and he returned in 1965 to New Orleans to play again. He toured Japan with George "Kid Sheik" Colar in 1967, and later, that same year, visited Europe with the Preservation Hall band.

MORE JAZZ GREATS FROM THE LOWLANDS

Gertrude Adam (piano)
Melba Adam (piano, vocals)
"Doc" Alphonse (guitar)
Tom Avery (saxophones, bass)
Joe Babin (trumpet)
Jules Babin (trombone, trumpet)
Tony Babin (trumpet)
Paul Barnes
Wilfred Bocage (saxophones, banjo)
Eldridge Butler (vocals)
George Clayborne (trombone)
Bill Crump (violin)
John Daniel (trumpet)
Jules Day (trumpet)
Minor Decou (clarinet)
Warnest Dequir (drums)
Clay Deroussell (bass)
Vick Despenses (trumpet)
Bernard Durea (vocals)
"Chup" Edwards (bass)
Tom Edwards (saxophone, bass)
Don Felton (drums)
Gus "Bubba" Fortinet, Jr. (alto sax)
Allen Gordon (guitar)
Alfred Grey (vocals)
Buster Hebert (banjo)
Sonny Hebert (bass)
Adam Jenkins
Lyles Johnson (trombone)
Buchanan Ledet (drums)
Baby Lovett (drums)
Nellie Lutcher (piano, vocals)
Skinner Lutcher (guitar, bass)
Zikka Mac (trumpet)
Albert Martel (trombone)
Burt Martel (trumpet)
Dayton Martel (trumpet, trombone)
Hillary Martel (violin)
Willie Martel (banjo)
Louis Masters (trumpet, bass)
Quintard Miller (violin)
Junius Nelson (vocals)
Claxton Norman (trumpet)
Professor Oger (trumpet)
The Pallot Brothers
Clasey Rov (saxophone)

Landers Roy (banjo)
Robert Stafford (drums)
Gardland Stewart (vocals)
"Tenance" (c-melody sax)
George Thomas (banjo)
Walter Thomas (drums)
Pierre Vital (bass)
Tim Vital (trumpet)
Louis Vitale (trombone)
Harold Walker (clarinet)
Alfraze Washington (trumpet)
Amerson Washington (trombone)
Hamilton Washington (trombone, banjo)

MILENBERG JOYS

Brightly

Milenberg Joys

Music by Leon Roppolo, Paul Mares and "Jelly Roll" Morton. Lyrics by Walter Melrose.

I CAN'T ESCAPE FROM YOU

I Can't Escape From You

From the Paramount Picture "Rhythm on the Range"

Words and Music by Leo Robin and Richard A. Whiting.

Main Street in Saint Martinville, Louisiana.

Hopkins Street in New Iberia, Louisiana.

"The Block" in Lafayette, Louisiana.

Breaux Bridge, Louisiana.

Bunk's home in New Iberia, Louisiana.

Bunk's grave. Inscription reads: "Here lies Willie "Bunk" Johnson. King of Horns. Prince of Jazz."